GIVE ME THE SIMPLE LIFE

By

Belinda Walker-Graham

ISBN: 1-4033-4062-5 (e-book)
ISBN: 1-4033-4063-3 (Paperback)

This book is printed on acid free paper.

1stBooks - rev. 08/14/02

DEDICATION

This book is dedicated to my loving husband Robert Graham for helping to make my dream come true with his patience and support. My son Ricardo L. Hofler Jr. for his encouraging words. My grandson Anthony. To all my family, especially my sisters: Billie Gloria and Pamela for listening to my dreams with no complaints. My brothers: Allan and Harold for believing in me. I love all of you very much. To all my dear friends, especially Michele for being supportive. To my mother-in-law Marilyn. My sister and bother-in-law Judy and Jimmy. Thank you for being a wonderful and supportive family.

ACKNOWLEDGMENT

In Loving Memory Of

My Parents Bernice and Harold Walker
My brother Larry Walker
My niece Kehia Shata Arleshia Walker

Special Thanks to my editor Bob Noonan for a job well done.

TABLE OF CONTENTS

If ever asked, as to why
life always take a turn

I'll simply say, in my own way
just what, I have learned

Life's a challenge we must meet
in any way we can

It will beat us down, until we fall
or lend a helping hand

Sick and tired, of life ups and downs
just makes me want to cry

Until something buried deep inside
keeps telling me to try

Life goes on, as we know
with all the pain and strife

But over and over, we ask, we pray
God Give Me The Simple Life

PROLOGUE

Atlanta, Georgia

At 12:30 in the afternoon, Veronica Winters walked to her car with an armful of balloons and presents. This was her last day of employment. Two weeks earlier she had handed in her resignation, with lots of reservations. Now the day had come, and the reservations she had felt were replaced with fear of the unknown. Very emotional from the day's event, she still managed a smile as she fantasized moving back to Michigan and surrounding herself with the people she loved, her family. Shaking off that euphoric feeling, she placed all the items in the car, and walked toward the front of the building. This had been her second home over the last three years.

Standing in front of the building brought back the memory of the first day she had reported to work here. It had been a gorgeous but hot day, and she was sweating bullets, due to the combination of heat and nerves. *So this is "hot lanta,"* she had said to herself, while shaking her blouse loose from the wetness of her skin. Walking towards the building with the sun beaming on her neck made her look up into the sky and thank God for having made it that far without passing out from heat exhaustion or a nervous breakdown. With the move, and getting settled in Atlanta, the stress had been almost unbearable, but she had persevered.

Returning back to the here and now, Veronica turned and walked to her car with a smile on her face. Thinking back on all the friends she had made, and the southern hospitality, she realized her stay here had been well worth it.

It was time to take that last drive back to her apartment. Driving through the gates of the apartment complex, Veronica felt a loss. She really was going to miss Atlanta. She shook the feeling off, parked, and went into the apartment for one last look. After taking a look around, she realized this was not home anymore. There was nothing but emptiness. All of her belongings were on their way to Michigan. Soon she would be, too.

Walking around the apartment brought back so many wonderful memories. Visits from her son Lamarr were always a joy. They had such a good relationship, the kind that all parents should have with their children.

And Preston. There were no words to describe the memories that would be left behind. Memories that would never fade away, even when new ones were made. The romantic evenings that are every woman's dream, sitting by the fireplace and dancing by the moonlight, were straight out of a movie. Finding him in her bed on one of his surprise visits would have won any woman's heart.

Jolted by a knock on the door, Veronica called out, "Who is it?"

"Maintenance, ma'am" a man's muffled voice said.

"I'm sorry," she replied, "but I didn't call maintenance. I'm moving out today."

Thinking the man was gone, Veronica started looking around to make sure she hadn't left anything behind. A second knock was heard. She looked out the door's peephole. With no one in view, she called out again, "Who is it?"

"Maintenance, ma'am. A repair call was made, I'm here to check it out."

"As I told you before, I'm moving out. There's been a mistake. You have the wrong apartment."

She was still looking out the peephole. Then a man came into view. With a hand over her mouth and widened eyes, she flung open the door and looked into the face of a handsome man with the most beautiful smile she'd ever seen.

After regaining her composure she said, pointing towards the empty room, "As you can see, I'm moving. I don't need maintenance. So why are you here?"

In a sexy baritone voice, he responded, "You may not need maintenance, but you do need me, just like I need you, desperately. I'm here to take you back home with me, where you belong."

CHAPTER ONE

I've always been impulsive, Ronnie thinks to herself, but I think this time I've gone too far. I actually quit my job of 22 years, with only eight years left to retirement.

And for what? I'm poor, no I'm poo without the r, and depending on a man to take care of me. I haven't done that since I was a child bride. Of course, then I didn't know any better. All I wanted to do was leave my mother, although I ended up with a father. I had an excuse for my stupidity back then. I was young. Now that I've reached 40 I'm supposed to be wise, or so they say. I think I made a liar out of whoever wrote that phrase. I couldn't have learned too much in my 40 years to have made such a life-changing decision as this. Although I have to admit, the change is refreshing. I really could get used to this.

The question is, can Preston? I feel so guilty watching him get up in the morning for work, and I'm lying in bed like a vegetable. Getting up is easy. Motivating myself to get busy and look for a job is not. Being content and not needing to look for work for the first time in many years has stagnated me. When it came to the job market, I had no idea what was going on in the real world. Looking for a job is a job. The only difference is, you're not getting paid. And I need to get paid fast!

Sometimes when I'm having a pity party, I'll pick up the phone to call my best friend Ashley. We were a comfort to each other when we both relocated to Atlanta. She'd say to me, "You had a job."

1

According to Ashley, I can't live without a man. Or should I say, without that part of the anatomy he has to offer. I have to admit, there's some truth to that statement. When Preston showed up in Atlanta pretending to be the maintenance man, he could have taken me to the moon, even though I'm petrified of flying. Knowing I would've had a heart attack before we even reached our destination, I would have gone anyway. But Preston wasn't the sole reason for the decisions I made. I really did need a change. I was totally burnt out. I only wish I'd realized how burnt out I was at age 35, when my butt was firmer and my breasts didn't droop as much. They're not down to my knees, but they can use a lift or two.

Alex, my older sister, thinks it's menopause. "Why else would you make such a rash decision?" she asks. Now this is coming from a woman who lives her life through books, which range from *Child-Rearing* to *What It Takes to Please Your Man*. She gets carried away sometimes, but she means well and I love her dearly. Since I moved back here to Michigan, she's always in my business. Always wanting to know what jobs I've looked into. When I suggested she should look into a job or two for herself, she almost choked on whatever she was stuffing into her mouth. Since marrying into money she has become comfortable playing the 'society woman,' and hosting parties for her husband's clients. Preparing for her calls has become mentally challenging, and it's around time for the phone to ring.

When it comes to predicting Alex, I'm right on the money. The phone just rang. I used to love talking on the phone. But since being unemployed, I hate hearing that ringing sound. Well, today I'm going to deviate from my normal routine. The answering machine can catch this one. Every time I run to catch a call, I'm disappointed when it's not a job opportunity.

The other day I ran to answer the phone, tripped, and knocked over the birdcage. The door opened and my bird Ivory flew out, and into the window. I guess she didn't realize it was glass. Knocked her out cold. When I bent down to take a look, my precious Ivory was gone. I went through all that only to hear, on the answering machine, the voice of my youngest sister, Paris, inquiring about my job search, and telling me how she's preparing to speak at a seminar on "Women in Business." She owns a travel agency, and instead of booking flights she wants to fly off the mouth on how I should go about finding a job. Which is cool, but she thinks she knows everything.

I'm glad I didn't catch her call because I would have accused her of murder. I buried my Ivory and made it back in time to catch my favorite soap, *It's Your Life*. Which is how I feel, but my sisters feel differently. So what if I gave up being a consultant to jumpstart a new life? I can do anything I want at any age, if I put my mind to it.

And that was confirmed by Leslie, my eldest sister. She always tries to find the good in everything and everyone. Even a murderer on death row. I value her opinion a lot, and I get it sometimes when I don't want it. But that's okay, I'll still listen. Sometimes I even take her advice.

Goodness, I must be popular today, because that phone is ringing off the hook again. Well, the machine can catch that one too, because I'm not moving from in front of this television set until a commercial comes on.

Curious about the call, I retrieve the message during a commercial. "Hey baby," he says. "Calling to find out how the love of my life is doing today. I miss you very much. I'm almost done with this case and should be home in the next day or so. And baby, I'm in need of some TLC. Love you."

"Tender Loving Care," my foot. A day or so. I return to Michigan and he leaves. The relationships I get myself into. I go from one extreme to another. Either the guy works too much, or doesn't work at all.

Being with a private investigator is like one day he's here, the next day he's gone. But when he's here, the sun forever shines, because he brings light into my life. That sounds pretty good, I must admit. Maybe I should take up poetry. I can write a lot of love poems, because I am definitely in love. I better be. I moved 726 miles to be with this man and start a new life. And he's not even in the state right now!

The thought of Preston being away puts me in a depressed mood. When you're depressed, you shop, I say, even when you don't have money. Shopping always cheers me up, and it's such a beautiful fall day. Michigan is bitter cold in the winter, but so beautiful towards the end of summer and into the fall, which is my favorite season. The temperature is just right, and the leaves turn the most beautiful colors.

I grab a light jacket and head out the door, humming. The traffic is light considering the time of day. Usually around 3 p.m. it's pretty heavy. Although you haven't seen heavy until you've been to Atlanta. I prayed everyday to make it home alive. Unfortunately, prayer didn't help the pedestrians. Some poor soul lost their life at least once a week. Walking on the streets of Atlanta is risking your life.

So much for reminiscing, I'm here at the Northland Mall. Gosh, it's been a long time. And nothing has changed. Crowded as ever and no parking space. I'll have to walk a mile parking in this spot. I shouldn't complain since I haven't worked out in a while, although Preston makes sure he keeps me active. But it's not enough. I'm tired already, and I've just begun.

Northland seems larger for some reason. Maybe it's because I have a lot of ground to cover and I'm too lazy to walk. Oh, that's my store! They have all the clothes you need to 'Dress for Success.' And I need success to come to me soon.

As I walk towards the store, not watching where I'm going, I bump into Gayla Martin. The woman who interviewed me for a management position last week. And who never called back, may I add.

"Hi Gayla, remember me? I'm Veronica Winters."

"Oh yes," she says. "I interviewed you for a position last week. How are you, my dear?"

"I'm doing fine. And how are you?"

"Very busy these days," she says. "Well, nice seeing you again Veronica."

I watch her walk away, frozen in my tracks, with my mouth hanging open. Not a word about the interview! I want to run after her, even fall on my knees and beg for a job. I'm not too proud to beg, you know. Instead I walk away with my head held high and strut back to my car. Shopping is not in the cards today.

I drive over to see Leslie. I need a perk-me-up, and Les is the only one who can meet that challenge. Leslie and her husband Steve live in a modest home in the Palmer Woods area. Turning down their street always brings on a calming effect for me. It's such a beautiful neighborhood, and peaceful.

As I pull into their drive, I see Les outside rearranging her flowerpots. During the summer, she goes to the pottery shop and buy her pots. And then heads to Eastern Market to buy various flowers. I'm not into the old plant and flower scene. A green thumb I don't have. But for Les, it's pure enjoyment. All the neighbors admire her arrangements, and even make offers to buy them. But Les always says no.

She looks up as I exit the car, and waves. "Hey Les," I say, "what's going on?"

"Hi Ronnie," she says. "As you can see, I'm rearranging my pots. And what brings you to my side of town?"

"I need a perk-me-up. Want to volunteer?"

"Sure, I can handle that. Why are you so down?"

"You wouldn't believe who I ran into at the mall. That's okay, don't even try to answer, because you'll never guess. Remember when I went to that interview for the position at Lynn's boutique?"

"You've been to so many," she says. "How do you expect me to remember?"

I put my hands on my hips and start telling Les what happened. "I bumped into that Gayla woman in the mall today. She was the person who interviewed me. Anyway she had the nerve to ask, 'How are you doing?'"

"Ronnie, what was she supposed to say?"

"How about, 'I apologize that I didn't get back to you.' Not, 'How are you?' I could have slapped her. She's not poor like me, with no job and almost homeless."

"Don't be over dramatic. Preston wouldn't put you on the streets unless money gets tight," she says, laughing.

"Very funny, Les. The next time that woman sees me, I'll be carrying a sign saying 'I'll work for food.'"

"Well, maybe someone will take notice and give you a job."

"You're full of it today, Les. If you start your own floral business, I can work for you."

"That's something I been thinking about doing."

"That's wonderful," I say, and tap her on the arm. "Girl, you have talent and people love your work. I was wondering when you were going to see it."

"I'm ready for a change in my life," she says. "I've been a wife and mother all my life, it seems. It's time to do what makes Leslie happy." She points a finger at her chest. "Everyone is doing their own thing. Steve runs his own business and the children are all grown up and living their own lives. I'm still young enough to start a career. But for some reason," she says, becoming suddenly sad, "Steve doesn't like the idea. I thought he'd be happy for me."

"Maybe he needs to get used to the idea that you want something different than he does."

"I don't know if that's it or not," she says. "Anyway I'll deal with it."

That's my cue to butt out. Les can give advice to the world, but when it comes to her accepting it from someone else, that's a different story. She'd rather handle her own problems.

"Well, Les," I say, "it's time for me to go home and check my machine. Maybe somebody wants me."

"Ronnie, the only one who wants you is Preston, whenever he's in town."

"On that note, I'll see you," I say, throwing up my hands.

While driving back home I start to chuckle, visualizing Les stacking her shelves with pots. She definitely won't need a ladder, that's for sure. And if anyone teases her about how tall she is, well all I can say is look out. At 5-feet 11-inches, she can beat anyone down.

Suddenly my smile fades, and I feel sadness. I'm worried about Les. She's usually so perky it's sickening. Maybe I'll give Alex a call when I get home. I need to find out if she knows what's going on with Les. Nah, I'll wait until tomorrow. Alex is probably busy reading that book, *How To Make Your Man Happy*. She feels that since she married into money, she needs to do everything right to keep her man. She's doing good so far without the book. Michael gives her everything she wants and needs. Although my sister is no dummy. Before she quit her job she put away enough money for a rainy day. Knowing Alex, she's going to make sure that rainy day doesn't come. I smile to myself as I enter my apartment complex.

"Welcome back to Michigan," I say aloud to myself.

CHAPTER TWO

"Alex, where's my navy blue suit?" Michael asks. "My plane leaves at 11:30 this morning, and my meeting starts around 2:30. There's not much time here. I need to leave for the airport soon and it's going to take an hour to get to the gate. Detroit Metro Airport is the worst in the country. I'll be the happiest man in the world when they finish renovating. Alex! Alex!"

"What, Michael?" she yells, coming into the room.

"My navy blue suit, sweetheart, have you seen it?"

"I took it to the cleaners, remember?" she tells him. "You didn't mention needing it for the trip."

"I'm sorry, sweetheart," he says. "My mistake. I'll wear the gray suit today. Sooo… Alex, what's on your itinerary for today?"

"I don't know. Maybe look for a part-time job."

"Not that again. How many times do I have to tell you that I don't want my wife working? I provide you with everything you need. A closet full of clothes, a Mercedes, and a beautiful home in Bloomfield Hills."

Seeing the disappointed look on her face, his tone softens. "Look sweetheart, you worked for years, and raised Simone by yourself. Now you can relax and let your Pookey take care of you. Come over here and give your Pookey a kiss."

Alex walks over and gives him a quick smack.

"That's my girl," he says. "Now, I need to finish getting ready."

Waiting until he leaves the room, she says in a low tone, "Pookey, I hate that name he gave himself. He couldn't even let *me* give him a pet name. Every time

9

he says that name, it reminds me of that crackhead Pookey in the movie *New Jack City*."

My life has become so boring, she says to herself. I have no hobbies to keep me occupied. Shopping has even become a bore. Maybe later I'll read that book I bought the other day, *How To Make Your Man Happy*. Staying at home should be at the top of the list, because it definitely does the trick for my man. I wonder what Ronnie's doing. Probably looking for dead-end jobs. That girl doesn't know anything about how to job-hunt. I'm beginning to think she doesn't want a job. If that's true, she's the one who should be married to Michael, not me. Well maybe she'll want to do lunch, since she has nothing else to do. We can swing around to Paris's office, pick her up, and go to that Arabic restaurant she loves so much.

"Sweetheart," Michael calls out from downstairs, "I'm ready to leave."

"Okay Michael," she says, "I'm on my way down."

When she reaches the foyer, she finds Michael standing by the door with his garment bag. "The meeting will last until around 7 tonight," he says, "and I'm sure we'll go for drinks. I'll probably get in too late to call. So I'll see you tomorrow, sweetheart." Noticing the look on her face, he makes a suggestion. "Why don't you go into the Glass Room, look out at the lake, relax, and read that book you don't want me to know about?" He gives her a big juicy kiss and walks out the door.

"I wonder what that's all about," she says out loud. "Those kind of kisses don't hit these lips too often. Like once a month."

Ah, she thinks, maybe Michael is right, as usual. All I need to do is relax and enjoy life. The Glass Room always brings me peace of mind. It's my favorite room, and the view is fantastic. Facing the lake with nothing but glass from the ceiling to the floor. And a step-up bar to boot. Decorated with turn of the century furniture, who wouldn't find comfort in that room? Or even be satisfied with all of this. Something must be wrong with me, or maybe menopause is kicking in big time. I'll skip lunch and call Les. Since mama passed away, Les has become her replacement. She didn't ask for the job, we gave it to her.

She walks over to the phone and punch in Les's number.

"Hey Les, what you doing?" Alex asks in a dry tone.

"Hi Alex. I'm sitting in the family room working on figures for my new business I'm starting."

"Business! What business?"

"I guess Ronnie didn't tell you. She came by all depressed, sounding somewhat like how you sound right now. Don't think I didn't pick up on that tone in your voice."

"I'm not depressed," Alex says. "What do I have to be depressed about?"

"You tell me," Les responds. "How am I supposed to know what's going on with you?"

"Well I'm not depressed, Les. On the other hand, Ronnie's always depressed about something. If it's not about that man of hers being out of town, it's about being jobless, homeless, or anything she can think of.

11

And to tell you the truth, I believe Preston the PI man is investigating, alright. Investigating another woman."

"Oh, come on, Alex. Why are you always thinking the worst? You know he has to go out of town for certain cases. He's a private investigator, for God sakes. It's his job."

"Okay Les, you don't have to keep going on and on. I get the picture. Anyway, that's their business. I have problems of my own."

"You do?" Les says, sounding sarcastic. "I thought you weren't depressed."

"Having problems doesn't always lead to depression. My problem is finding a part-time job."

"How is that a problem, Alex? If that's what you want, go for it."

"Les, you know Michael would have a hissy fit. He feels I should stay at home and let him take care of me."

"I think control is a better word," Les comments. "Where's your spunk, Alex? You use to be a go-getter, no one could tell you what to do. What happened?"

"I don't know." She sighs. "I guess I don't want to rock the boat."

"Well Alex, I suggest you continue to read that book so you can rock his world. Speaking of rocking his world, I gotta go and spend some time with Steve. I'm sure right about now he's feeling neglected."

"Okay girl, talk to you later," Alex says, and hangs up.

She walks over to look out at the lake. What am I to do next? she wonders. Life should be more exciting than this. I miss my husband so much. When he's here, he's not really here. He's always involved in his work.

If he was here both mentally and physically more often, I wouldn't be so lonely and bored. Even if he doesn't think so, I do understand that he has big responsibilities being a senior partner with Hinds & Crawford. He's either in court or traveling.

Like today, I'm sure he could have assigned another attorney to handle this merger. But noo... he felt it's too important. That he's the only one experienced enough to make this deal go through. "My clients need pampering," he says. Well, I need pampering too! Sometimes I wonder if it's always business. No, I can't allow myself to think that way. If I had a job to occupy my mind, I wouldn't have time to conjure up thoughts like this.

A knock on the door interrupts her thoughts. It's Doris, the maid.

"Yes, Doris," Alex says, "what is it?"

"I'm sorry to disturb you, but Mrs. Findley is here to see you."

"Send her up to the Glass Room, and thank you Doris."

"Yes ma'am," Doris says, and leaves.

"Hey sis," Alex says as Paris comes through the door "What brings you to Bloomfield Hills?"

"I was in the area. I had to take care of some business and thought I'd swing by."

"And how is business?"

"Girl, business is booming," Paris answers. "I've picked up quite a few clients."

"And quite a few outfits," Alex adds. "Look at you. That's a sharp suit, and with shoes to match. Looking good. I see you're wearing your hair down, too."

"Yeah, I thought a change would do some good," she says. "And Neil loves my hair down."

"How are you two lovebirds doing?"

"Since getting back together, things couldn't be better."

"You both had a year of separation to think things through."

"I know, and I was miserable without him, even when I found another lover. It just wasn't the same."

"Of course it wouldn't be the same. You were still in love with your husband. Leonard was only a substitute. If Neil hadn't gone off on a coochie hunt, you wouldn't have given Leonard or anyone else a second thought."

"All I can say is, 'It feels good to be back with my baby,'" Paris sings.

"I guess it would be after being with Leonard, the wannabe Rapper," Alex comments. "What attracted you to that, as prissy as you are? He's cute and all, but goodness, his pants were never on his butt."

"Girl, I was quite vulnerable when I met him."

"You may have been vulnerable, but how could you overlook the obvious? The man had a gold tooth, for God sakes, and he drove a Pinto. Where in the world did he find a Pinto? No one drives a Pinto!"

"Okay Alex, enough," Paris says, laughing and holding her hands over her ears. "Leonard is a thing of the past. Neil and I are back on track. He doesn't have to fly overseas anymore. All of his flight plans are in the U.S. of A." She pauses. "I have to confess something to you."

Alex's eyes widen and she sits still, listening intently.

"At one point," Paris says, "before Neil and I separated, I almost asked Preston to do some PI work for me."

"Really!" Alex is surprised.

"Yep, sure did. I wanted to know what was going on. Neil started volunteering for certain flights on his days off. Always to Houston."

"Did you ever ask him about it?"

"What do you think?" Paris says, with confusion on her face. "Do you actually think a man will tell you he's messing around?"

"You're right. So how did you find out?"

"Well, Neil told me he had an early flight on a Wednesday. Something about how one of the pilots had an emergency. He told me about his flight plans, like normal. That night I called up a different airline and booked a flight to Houston early enough to get there before him. After I arrived, I waited in a cab until I saw him come out. I had my cab to follow the cab he was in. When he reached his destination, I had my cab driver pull over, and I sat and watched.

"Miss Thang jumped out of her car when she saw Neil's cab pull up. Alex, she was running to greet Neil in this hoochie mama dress. Her shoes must have been too tight, because she was running like her feet were hurting. May I add, that comes from cheap shoes too. Anyway they were hugging and kissing right there in the street. So I had the cab driver pull up next to them. The driver acted like he didn't want to do it, but he did."

"Girl," Alex observes, "that man didn't know what you were up to. I would have been leery too. For all he knew, you could have been plotting to commit murder."

"Little did he know, I wanted to," Paris says. "But my boys needs a father, and that tramp wasn't worth it. When the cab driver pulled up next to them, I jumped out of the cab and caught them both by surprise. I kicked Neil in the nuts and pulled some of Miss Thang's braids out. I made sure Neil wasn't going to get his groove on that night. And for Miss Thang, she needed her hair redone anyway. I yanked so hard I'm sure I pulled out what little hair she had."

"What did you do next?" Alex asks, fascinated.

"I ran for my life," Paris says. "I didn't even have to tell the cab driver to step on it. As soon as I jumped in the cab, girl, that man took off! I stuck my head out of the window and threw up my middle finger at Neil and Miss Thang."

"Girl, give me a high five!" Alex says. "You didn't need Preston, Miss PI."

"I know, I'm too good," she grins.

"Maybe you can teach me a trick or two," Alex tells her. "I'm beginning to wonder if all of Michael trips are business related. He's gone all the time. I'm getting so lonely and bored."

"Why don't you give Ronnie a call?" Paris says. "Find out when Preston is returning."

"Nah, I think all I need is something to do. I'm letting my imagination run wild."

"Alex, your husband have more money than he knows what to do with. Talk to him about starting a business. You always wanted to open a boutique."

"That's what I'll do as soon as he returns. I can't see why Michael would object to that."

"I can't either, sis. But right now, I must cut this visit short. I love chatting with you, but I have a dinner date with my husband."

"I'm glad you stopped by, you made my day."

They hug and give an affectionate kiss to each other. Alex doesn't want Paris to leave, because she'll be alone again. After shutting the door behind Paris, Alex leans her head back, hoping she'll hear from Michael tonight.

Walking back into the Glass Room makes her feel at peace again. "I need to feel as if Michael is here with me, she says out loud. "I'll put on Rochelle Ferrell's CD. Michael loves that woman. We used to spend at lot of time together in this room, making love to her songs. Meeting Michael was like a dream come true. He's intelligent, successful, and has the look of a man very secure within himself. He's not drop-dead gorgeous, but he wear his suits well."

While the music plays, she starts reminiscing about how she met Michael, and their marriage.

I'd been at the 36th District Court testifying on behalf of my employer. A client was suing the company due to breach of contract. Michael was the attorney on behalf of the Plaintiff. His firm handled mergers, contract disputes, and so forth. He won the case for his clients. And I won a date.

As I was leaving the building after the case, I heard someone call my name. I turned around to see Michael running with his brief case, trying to catch me before I left the building.

"I wanted to apologize," he'd said. "I was pretty tough on you in the courtroom."

I knew it was an excuse to talk to me, so I played along. "That's your job," I said. "You were very smooth."

He smiled, showing those big pretty dimples, and said, "Let's have lunch."

The way he asked, I was sure he expected me to say yes, and I decided to put him in his place. "I'm sorry," I said, "but unfortunately I have a previous engagement."

"Well, may I have your number and a rain check?" he asked, still smiling.

I reached into my purse and pulled out my business card. Smiling back, I said, "I hope you make use of this number," and handed the card to him.

He looked down at my card and said, "I most certainly will." He placed the card in his wallet, lifted his head up and told me to have a good day, and walked away.

As I walked to my car I smiled to myself, and said, "This is the one."

But five days passed, and no call. I was beginning to think my instincts had failed me. I continued my daily routine, with the exception of checking my voice mail more often. Michael was beginning to act like all the other men I'd encountered. Make promises and not keep them.

By the following week I'd given up hope. Then, to my surprise, he called, apologizing profusely for not having called sooner. Apparently, he'd had to go out of town unexpectedly.

We had a wonderful conversation, and made arrangements for dinner. We decided to meet at the New Center area and go to dinner from there.

I wanted to impress Michael on our first date, so I went shopping for a new dress. It was plain, but it made a statement. My pearl necklace and earrings added a touch of class, which he had plenty of. On the day of our date my hair was perfect, not a strand out of place. Standing in the mirror, looking myself over, I said out loud, "Girl you are absolutely gorgeous."

Everything was perfect, and we looked good together. Michael was a gentleman, and displayed more humor than I thought he had. Since dinner was a success, we decided to continue the night. I told him about a quaint little jazz club, Downtown Detroit, and he was all for going. I left my car parked and rode with Michael.

Inside the jazz club we enjoyed each other's company immensely. I thought about recommending a dance club, but the way Michael moved to the beat, I decided against it. A thought came to my mind; was Michael's lack of rhythm limited to the dance floor? I was sure I'd find out in due time.

We tried to talk over the music but it was impossible, so we left and went to a coffee shop. Michael was very talkative, which didn't surprise me, given his profession. I couldn't get a word in. I didn't mind really, because I wanted to know all about this man. And I got an ear full.

He explained how he became interested in the Criminal Justice System. His parents were both Circuit Court judges. They lived in Palisades Park in Arlington, Virginia, but commuted daily to Washington, D.C. Both were originally from Detroit. His mother, he said, was very domineering, and interfered too much in his personal life. So he chose to put some distance between them, and move back to Detroit.

All of a sudden he changed the subject to other things. I knew then that his mother was someone to contend with.

The night was finally coming to a close, but I knew I wanted to see him again. And it was confirmed that he felt the same way, when he asked if I had plans for the next day. My heart was beating so fast I was afraid he could see my dress move. I kept my composure and said yes.

That was the beginning. After that night, we started spending as much time together as his job would allow.

The closer we got, the more controlling he became. I gradually allowed him to strip me of my identity and independence. At first, strange as it seemed, I liked it. I was getting all of this attention, which meant to me that he really loved me. He showered me with gifts and weekend trips when he could get away.

I saw all the warning signs but ignored them. I was no teenager, and I knew better. I guess that getting older and wanting someone to grow old with, interfered with my better judgment. When he asked me to marry him, I was so happy. But those inner feelings were telling me not to go into this marriage half stepping.

I needed to talk to him about how I felt, but there was never time after I started getting involved with the wedding plans. Then there was his job, which took up a lot of his time. We did make time to fly to Arlington to meet his parents, my future in-laws. That was a total disaster. They were cordial, of course. But Mrs.

Crawford made me feel like I wasn't good enough for her precious Michael. On the other hand, Mr. Crawford was very nice, more down to earth.

Meeting Michael's parents was a good thing for more reasons than one. It gave me insight into why Michael was so controlling. His mother Beatrice was a real Gestapo. She ruled that house, including poor James, Michael's father. I actually saw the man flinch when Beatrice demanded they go to Martha's Vineyard on their vacation that year.

When asked about my family background, I politely informed Mrs. Crawford my parents were deceased, and I'd rather not talk on that subject. Feeling snubbed, Beatrice ignored me for the rest of the night, which was fine with me. Beatrice then turned her attention to Michael.

For some reason Michael seemed a bit uncomfortable around his mother. I didn't see any kind of loving relationship there, although I was sure it existed. After all, they were mother and son.

As we all proceeded to the study for coffee, I noticed a portrait of Mrs. Crawford hanging in the hallway. She was all alone in the painting, there was no other family member with her. I thought that was very strange. As a matter of fact, I saw no pictures of Beatrice's husband, and only a few of Michael. It made me wonder if this woman had any love at all in her heart. Or had something happened to make her so miserable?

The only enjoyable moment was the tour of their beautiful home. Mrs. Crawford excused herself to take a call, so Mr. Crawford and Michael did the honors. I was given the history of the magnificent place, and the meaning behind all the collectibles they had. I felt like a princess in a castle, until the thought of that mean old witch residing there destroyed my fantasy.

After the tour, we bid our goodnights and left for the hotel. Michael apologized for his mother's behavior. Those were the last words he spoke for the rest of the night. I didn't question him. I felt when he was ready to talk about it, he'd come to me. But he hasn't, to this very day.

The tension between Michael and his mother showed during our wedding. I noticed it, although no one else did.

Beatrice tried to take over. She told everyone what to do, and how to do it. Michael stood in the background and watched with an angry expression. Beatrice was busy making her way through the crowd, greeting the people he had invited and actually laughing. One would have thought she was a saint. But I knew the woman was really a barracuda.

Beatrice also snubbed my family. I was not going to tolerate it and was ready to take action, but Ronnie beat me to the punch.

Mrs. Crawford was trying to tell everyone what to do. She insisted that I keep my mouth shut and let Michael do all the talking, because I wasn't polished enough. I was livid. But before I could open my mouth, Ronnie was in the woman's face.

"Look, you old battleaxe," she said. "I suggest you back off, or I'll embarrass you in front of all of your society friends. And another thing, you give my sister and our family the respect you want in return. I hope I made myself clear."

Mrs. Crawford stood with her mouth open and a hand on her chest, speechless. When she regained her composure, she looked straight at Ronnie. "I wouldn't waste words on you my dear," she said. "You wouldn't understand them anyway." With a smirk on her face, she turned and walked out.

Les had to pull Ronnie back before she grabbed the old woman and beat her down. Paris stood on the side laughing so hard, we had to redo her makeup from the tears.

I remember thinking: Nothing fazes that old women. I'm in for a ride.

The wedding went off smoothly, and we started our lives together, without his mother in it. Not that she didn't try to meddle. But what could she do from Arlington, Virginia?

Sometimes I can see the longing for a mother's love in Michael's eyes. I wondered if that would ever happen.

Alex snaps back into the present. "What's more important," she announces with sudden determination, "is, how are we going to get back on track? Our marriage is in serious trouble."

As she sips on a glass of wine and continues to reminisce, the ring of the phone jars her. She picks it up, to hear a familiar and welcomed voice.

Belinda Walker-Graham

CHAPTER THREE

"Steve, we've gone over this before. Don't you understand? I need to do this." Leslie is getting frustrated.

"Why, Les? Don't I make you happy? Look, baby, if you start your own business, you won't have time for me. We won't be able to do all the things we used to do."

"I know, Steve," she says. "But once I get the business off the ground, we can start to do more things together. I have to concentrate on this right now."

"So already you're putting the business before me?"

"Are you that insecure, Steve? Do you feel threatened?"

"I have my own business," he answers. "But it's our money. You don't have to want for anything. You or the children never went without."

"Don't you think I know that? And I love you for it," she points out. "But this is not about you. It's about me. Can't you try to understand? Let's drop this conversation, because it always lead to an argument. I want us to spend some quality time together."

"I want the same thing," he says. "But I must tell you Les, this conversation is far from over."

She watches Steve walk out of the room and then out the door. "If he think I'm giving up my dream, he just better think again," she says out loud. "I'm a new woman now, and I'm going to jump right into this with a vengeance."

To herself she says: I have a lot to prove, mainly to myself. I'm capable of being more than just a housewife and mother. I was very smart in school. Just because I didn't go to college doesn't mean I'm not smart enough to run a business. I'll take classes on how to run a small business. Whatever it takes to succeed. Little does he know the lengths I've gone through already. I've researched through the internet, and read books on how to start a business. I know I can do this. And like Ronnie says, I have talent. Now all I have to do is put this talent to work. Anyway, Steve and I have come to a crossroad. Occupying my time in a constructive way will compensate for the boredom I've been feeling lately. This means more than achieving a goal I've set for myself. It could very well save a marriage he's not even aware is in jeopardy.

I love Steve very much. He came into my life at a time when I needed someone to lean on. I was going through a divorce and trying to raise April and Randall on my own. I've always wanted to be married, so the divorce was a big blow to me. My dream of growing old with my husband and raising our family together was destroyed. And so was I. Depression set in, and I was no good to my children or myself. Then Steve came into the picture. The children took to him right away. He had no children of his own, so he treated my children like they were his. After we married he wanted to adopt them, but that was out of the question. They already had a father, and he was very much in their lives.

Steve is a good man, a loving husband and father. Right now he's confused. He's not sure of me anymore. I can't expect him to change his way of thinking because I've changed mine. It would be very selfish of me not to try to understand how he feels. After all, he's used to the way things have been for years. And it's going to take time for him to accept the change in our lives.

Steve interrupts Les's train of thought, and she becomes irritated. "What is it, Steve?" she yells. "I thought you went outside."

"Pick up the phone!" he yells back. "It's Ronnie. And as I recall, this is my house also. And I chose to come back inside!"

She walks over to pick up the phone with a frown on her face.

"Hi Les," Ronnie says. "Did I catch you at a bad time?"

"No, I was sitting in the kitchen, thinking."

"A penny for your thoughts," Ronnie responds.

"You can't get off that cheap," she laughs. "I was thinking how things changes, and how nothing stays the same."

"Oh God, would you want them to? If everything stays the same, there'd be no progress. We wouldn't become any wiser. Although I wonder about some folks, including myself. But can you imagine wearing afro puffs forever?"

"No Ronnie, I can't. I didn't wear them when they were in fashion, you did," Les reminds her.

"Oh, that's right," she says. "I spoke with Alex earlier today."

"What was she doing?"

"Nothing, as usual. Trying to read that book, and missing Michael all at the same time."

"Michael's out of town again?"

"Yep, and I think Alex is getting a little tired of him being gone so much. She's lonely, Les."

"Maybe we all need to go out to dinner," Les suggests. "We can all use some cheering up."

"Okay, that sounds good to me. I'll call Paris to let her know. By the way, Paris stopped by Alex's today."

"She did?"

"Yep, and she told Alex all about how she busted Neil in Houston."

"Oh, I remember, when she flew to Houston and didn't tell anyone where she was going." Les had never gotten the details.

"That was the time," Ronnie responds. "She followed Neil to that woman's place by cab. Then she jumped out of the cab, kicked Neil in the groin and pulled the woman's braids out."

"Get out of here! No, she didn't!"

"Yes she did," Ronnie says, laughing. "You know, Paris can become a wild animal when pushed."

"Very much so," Les agrees. "So Ronnie, when is Preston returning?"

"Tomorrow, and boy do I have a surprise for him."

"Well I hope you two have big fun," Les says, with a little sadness.

"You know we will. Are you okay, Les?"

"I'm fine, just a little distracted. I'm doing my normal routine, which is housecleaning. I better get off this phone so I can get it over with."

"Alright, if you must," she says. "I don't want to stop progress."

"Very funny, Ronnie. I'll call you, not tomorrow of course."

"You better not," she says. "Even if you did, I wouldn't answer."

"Good-bye Ronnie," Les says, laughing, and hangs up.

Ronnie's in a good mood, Les thinks to herself. Preston is good for her. But I don't know how good Michael is for Alex. I hate seeing my sister so unhappy. I wonder why Michael's out of town so much. Maybe it's only business, and Alex is worrying over nothing. I'll give her a call tomorrow.

In the meantime, I need to get a handle on my own situation. I have trouble here at home. I bet Steve is downstairs, on the internet. That's been his pastime lately.

After Steve retired, we traveled all the time. We spent so much time together. Now we rarely spend any time together, or even communicate. I should be more considerate of his feelings. No more conversing over the phone tonight. I'm going downstairs to give my husband some much needed attention. I'll tiptoe down the stairs and surprise him with a nibble on the ear.

When she reaches the bottom steps, a creaking sound startles him. "Leslie," he yells, "you almost gave me a heart attack! Don't sneak up on me like that!"

She looks over at the computer, and becomes speechless. Finally she says, "Steve, what is this? What's going on here?"

"Les, I was just searching the internet and stumbled on this. It's not like I was looking for it."

"I don't believe you, and don't play stupid with me! You knew what you were looking for. What, I'm not enough for you now?"

"Don't be silly, Les," he says. "You're getting a little carried away here. It's only porn. We use to watch it together, remember? Why all of a sudden it's a big deal?"

"It's a big deal," she tells him in no uncertain terms, "because we're having problems, and no sex. And you find it necessary to get your rocks off watching women over the internet. You have the real thing right here and don't want it. How into this are you? I mean, how often do you watch this trash?"

"Oh it's trash now? I guess since you're becoming a business woman, this is beneath you."

"Why don't you grow up," she says. She's mad now. "It's a floral shop, not a law firm I'm opening. I don't want to discuss this anymore."

"That's what you always say, and then walk away," he responds. "You can't finish anything you start. Like this so-called business. It's only a pipe dream. And you're going to be dreaming forever."

Tears are rolling down Les's face now. "That's it!" she yell. "Go ahead and do your own thing, and I'll do mine. But when I finish, you'll see how much of a pipe dream it really is." With that, she turns and runs up the stairs.

"Damn," Steve says, frustrated. "I'm not going out looking for sex, I'm just watching it." Then he says, "Who am I kidding? Les is trying to grow, and I'm trying to hold her back. She's not that same dependent woman I married years ago. But then again, I'm not the same either. No matter how I try, I'll never be the same again."

Upstairs, Les washes her face and wonders what's really happening. She thinks: This is not like Steve. And why is he so reluctant for me to start a business? Something else must be going on.

Mentally exhausted, she climbs into bed and drifts off into a deep sleep. Awakened by a disturbing dream, she realizes it's daylight. She also notices the space next to hers is empty. Steve didn't come to bed last night.

Suddenly he appears from out of the bathroom. "Good morning," he says.

When she doesn't answer Steve walks over to the bed and sits down. "I'm sorry about last night," he says.

"What you said to me last night hurt," she responds.

"I didn't mean to cause you pain," he says. "Please forgive me."

Not giving a response, she slides out of bed and heads towards the bathroom. Stopping, she turns to face him. "Right now I need some space to think, if you don't mind."

Steve nods, then stands up and walks towards the bedroom door to leave. "I do love you," she mumbles. He stops for a second, then walks out.

I refuse to turn back now, she says to herself. Now, more than ever I'm determined to make my dream come true.

Off into her own thoughts, she doesn't hear the phone ring. Finally, after the fourth ring she snaps out of it and runs to catch the call.

"Oh, Mr. Langley," she says. "I didn't recognize your voice at first. How are you?"

"I'm fine Mrs. Wade," he answers. "I'm returning your call. I assume you're still interested in renting my building?"

"Yes I am Mr. Langley. Is it still available?"

"Yes it is. And if you want to come over and take a look, I'm available tomorrow around noon."

"I can definitely make it at that time," she says excitedly.

"Good," he says. "I look forward to seeing you tomorrow Mrs. Wade. Good-bye."

She hangs up the phone, then screams in excitement. "I can't wait to tell my sisters! It's happening! Oh please, please God, let it be affordable."

I've saved up quite a bit of money over the last three years, she says to herself. Of course I didn't know it would be used for this. I just wanted to have a personal account so I could feel independent. Every cent Steve gave me, I put away. I have enough to cover the rent for at least six months, and also utilities and all the necessities needed to run my business. At least until I see the profits roll in. Oh, this is great! I guess now I should start speaking to Steve again, since I need him. He's an electrician and can look over the building for me. That's if I can get him to come. With his attitude these days, it may be hard to convince him. If he doesn't want to come, so be it. I'll ask Paris.

That's it, Paris would be a better choice. She started her own business and would know the proper questions to ask. Then I'll ask Michael to look over the contract.

"Girl, you got it going on!" Les says out loud as she calls Paris.

"Hey Paris, my favorite sister!"

"What's up Les?" Paris asks. "You either want something or you got a piece this morning."

"Oh hush," she says. "I got some great news."

"You hit the lotto," Paris says. "And you want to share it with me. How sweet."

"No, silly, I think I have a building for my floral shop."

"What floral shop?" she asks.

"Oh, I forgot to tell you," Les says. There's silence on the other end. "I was going to tell you."

"Sure you were," she says. "If it wasn't for the fact that you need something from me, I would not have known."

"Come on, Paris. Be a nice sister."

"What is it, Les?"

"I need you to go with me tomorrow around noon to talk to the landlord. Will you go? Please, please, please?"

"Oh I love it when you beg," she laughs. "You know I'll go with you. That's wonderful news and it will be my pleasure to help my big sister. But why isn't Steve going?"

"He's busy," Les lies.

"About us getting together for dinner," Paris comments. "It's cool with me. I need some time for myself and away from Neil and the twins."

"Okay, we'll talk more on that tomorrow. Talk to you later, sis."

As soon as Les hangs up the phone, it rings. Now who is this? she wonders. I'll never get my day started talking on the phone.

"Hello," she answers.

33

"Hi, this is Ann from Dr. Richard's office."

"Ann, how are you?"

"I'm fine Mrs. Wade. And how are you this beautiful day?"

"Couldn't be better," Les says. "What can I do for you this morning?"

"I'm calling to confirm Mr. Wade's appointment for tomorrow," she answers. "It's at 9:30."

"Mr. Wade is out right now," Les responds. "But I'll make sure he gets the message."

"Thank you," Ann replies. "Have a good day."

Les slowly removes the phone from her ear in a state of shock, then eases down into her chaise lounge. This is not like Steve, she thinks, to make a doctor's appointment without telling me. It's so out of character. My instinct tells me something is wrong. And that call confirms it. I thought his behavior was about my starting a business. But it seems to be more about him than me. Have I been that out of touch, to the point I couldn't see my husband's health failing?

Everything has gotten out of control. Steve didn't even come to me and discuss his problem. Since he's so closed-mouth about what's going on, I'll try to get it out of Dr. Richards. Maybe he'll provide me with some answers.

Les grab something out of the closet to put on and heads downstairs. On her way out the door, she stops and picks up their wedding picture. Looking at the picture lovingly, she wonders how could this be happening to them. We had close to a perfect marriage, she muses, more perfect than anyone I know. She place the picture back on the table and walks out the door.

While backing out the drive, she almost hits the car coming down the street. She slams on the brakes and takes a deep breath. I've got to calm down, she tells herself.

On the way to the doctor's office she has all kinds of thoughts. What if it's some incurable disease? I couldn't handle losing him. No, I can't allow myself to think such thoughts.

While pulling into the parking lot, she notices Steve's car turning out onto Ten Mile Road. What in the world is he doing here? she wonders. Knowing Steve, he wanted to make sure the office didn't call our house to confirm his appointment. I wonder if Ann told him she called. I can't worry about that right now. I'll deal with that later. Right now I need answers.

She parks and exits the car. Upon entering the crowded office, she looks around, takes a deep breath, and proceeds to walk up to the receptionist desk.

"Hello Mrs. Wade," Ann says. "I don't see you on the books today."

"I'm not," Les answers. "I need to speak with Dr. Richards. I won't need much time."

"I'm sorry Mrs. Wade," she says. "As you can see, the doctor has a busy schedule."

"This is important Ann," Les whispers. "It will only take about 15 minutes. Would you please ask Dr. Richards if he can spare a few minutes? Please?"

"I'll check with the doctor," Ann says. "But I can't guarantee he'll see you."

"Thank you Ann," Les says. "I really appreciate this. By the way, did Mr. Wade stop into the office today?"

"Not that I'm aware of," Ann responds, with a puzzled look. "If Mr. Wade did come into the office, it could have been during the time I stepped out for lunch. I can ask Ms. Jefferson."

"No, that won't be necessary."

"I'll return shortly," Ann says.

As soon as Les starts to sit down, Ann returns. "The doctor will see you," she states. "However, the patients come first."

"I don't mind waiting," Les replies. "I'll take a seat and wait to be called." Ann nods and closes the sliding window.

Les takes the only seat available, next to a little old lady who looked sweet but is very feisty. This woman is all into the soap opera on the television set. She's cursing and yelling at the characters as if they could hear her. Les wonders, Who would have known this sweet little old lady could out-curse a sailor?

When the commercial comes on the woman turns to Les. "I love this soap don't you?" she asks.

"No I don't," Les answers. "As a matter of fact, it's the worst soap on TV."

"You're a very mean woman," the old lady says, very loud. Heads turned towards Les as if she's beating up on the woman. Les thinks, I guess God don't like ugly. What's wrong with me? I'm always sociable. I get along with everyone, but right now I'm out of control.

"Mrs. Wade," the nurse calls. Les stands up. "The doctor will see you now. Please come with me."

Les follows the nurse through the door and is directed to Dr. Richards' office. A minute or two later,

Dr. Richards enters. "Well hello Leslie," he says. "What brings you in today?"

"Hi Martin," she says. "Thanks for seeing me on short notice. I know you're busy, so I'll get right to the point. It's about Steve. What's wrong with him, Martin?"

Dr. Richards doesn't respond. Which makes Les a little uncomfortable, and she moves around in her chair.

"I know he made an appointment with you for tomorrow," she says. "Steve always tell me his appointments, or when he's not feeling well. Which leads me to believe something is wrong. Can you please shed some light on this?"

"It true Leslie," he says. "Steve did make an appointment with me."

"Tell me something I don't know," Les responds.

"Leslie, I'm sorry, but that's as far as I can go. I don't have to explain to you about doctor and patient confidentiality. You're well aware of that."

The look of disappointment on Les's face makes Dr. Richard's tone soften. He seats himself and begins to explain further.

"Look Leslie," he says. "You and Steve have been under my care for almost 20 years. I understand your concern, but I can't divulge any information about Steve even if he is your husband. Go home, Leslie, and talk to Steve. I'm sure if it's something you need to know, he'll tell you."

"I'm sorry Martin," she says. "I didn't mean to put you on the spot."

"Leslie, anytime you need to talk or have questions, please don't hesitate to stop by or call. I

37

may not have all the answers, but I will take time out of my schedule to accommodate you."

They both stand up. Dr. Richards walks over to Leslie and places a hand gently on her shoulders. "Don't worry," he says reassuringly.

Leslie thanks him again and leaves. On her way home all she can think about is approaching Steve about this.

My husband must be afraid, she says to herself, and dealing with this all alone. The floral shop is very important to me, but my husband is more important. I must make him my number one priority. The first thing I'm going to do is cancel my appointment with Mr. Langley. I need to spend time with Steve. I'll arrange to see the building at another time. Then, I need to call Paris and cancel. I hope it's not a problem with rescheduling. If so, I'll look into finding another building to rent. I've waited this long, and I'll wait longer if necessary.

Pulling into the drive, Les notices Steve isn't there. She lets out a sigh of relief. Good, she thinks, he's not home yet. I can cool out a little bit and call Mr. Langley.

After Les enters the house, she goes straight to the family room and flops down onto the sofa. Not able to relax, she gets up and walks toward the phone to call Mr. Langley. She dials the number, then, having second thoughts, she starts to hang up. But before she can, Mr. Langley answers.

"Hello Mr. Langley," she says, "this is Mrs. Wade."

"Well hello again," he says. "I have the pleasure of talking to you twice today."

"I'm calling to see if we can reschedule our appointment," she says.

"I'm sorry Mrs. Wade, but that's going to be impossible," he responds. "I set up all my appointments for tomorrow only. The building has been listed about three months now. Several people including yourself, Mrs. Wade, have expressed a strong interest in renting the building. I'll make my decision after speaking with each individual tomorrow."

"I understand Mr. Langley," she says quietly.

"Then I'll see you tomorrow around noon?"

"Yes, you will," she answers.

Nothing is going right for me today, she says to herself after hanging up the phone. I'm mentally exhausted. If I had the courage, I'd book a room for the night. A different atmosphere would ease the tension, even if it's only for one night.

Turning to go upstairs for a hot bath, Les bumps into Steve. "Goodness, Steve!" she says. "You scared me. I didn't hear you come in."

"You were on the phone," he says. "I went into the kitchen for a snack, then upstairs. I also found the note confirming my appointment for tomorrow."

"Is everything all right, Steve?"

"I'm fine Les," he answers. "I've been having back pains and thought I should get it checked out."

"I can go with you," she offers.

"That won't be necessary," he responds. "Anyway you have an appointment yourself concerning that building."

"I didn't tell you about that," she says.

"I overheard you asking Paris to go with you."

39

"How? I called Paris after you left. Are you spying on me?"

"No I'm not," he says, raising his voice. "I was halfway down the block and realized I didn't have my wallet. I entered our home the way I normally would," he says with emphasis. "You were into your conversation. I guess you didn't hear me."

"I was rather excited," she says. "I'm sorry I accused you of spying."

"Are you also going to apologize for not having enough faith in me?"

"What do you mean, Steve?"

"Les, you didn't think I had the smarts to talk to this guy, did you? So you asked Paris to go with you, instead."

"I asked Paris because she has a business. So it's only logical I would want her with me. You have showed little to no interest in what I'm doing."

"You have an answer for everything don't you?" he says, obviously irritated.

Les opens her mouth to answer, but nothing comes out. Steve looks at her and walks away.

Well I blew that one, she says to herself. So much for being sensitive. What I need now is a stiff drink, so I can be oblivious to the world.

Give Me the Simple Life

Belinda Walker-Graham

CHAPTER FOUR

As Ronnie runs around the apartment getting things in order, she's singing Barry White's song, *Practice What You Preach*. She thinks, I love it when he sings the part on how it's so many ways he can please. Ooh, that man gets my juices flowing. Preston is in for a treat. If only I can get into finding a job like I can seducing my man, I'd be working right now.

Let's see, who should I be tonight? I like Preston to feel he's with a different woman sometimes. And he seems to love it. Variety is the spice of life, they say. Where are my candles? Oh here they are. Champagne bubble bath and body oil is accounted for. All I need is for Preston to be here. I miss him so much.

There was a time when I wouldn't give Preston the time of day.

Our first meeting, or clash, I should say, was during a routine traffic stop. Preston was a police officer for Oakland county. I was on my lunch hour, trying to do too many things. I was doing 60 in a 50 mph zone on Telegraph Road. When I heard the siren, I pulled into the nearest gas station. Out stepped this fine officer, about 6-feet 4-inches. He looked so good in his uniform, and was the perfect height. For me, it was like a dream come true. I'm 5-feet 10-inches and taller than most men I meet, especially when I'm wearing heels. My parents were tall, so it was inevitable that their children would be too. And we all are.

When this officer started walking towards the vehicle, I'm thinking, I can get out of this one. But when he reached the vehicle, he looked so serious and started explaining the reason he stopped me. I knew at that moment I was doomed, but I was still going to put forth my best efforts. As he talked I stared him straight in the eyes, and put on that sultry look.

It would have worked, but the problem came when I was asked to hand over my license and registration. I reached over for my purse, and it wasn't there. I looked all around the car, at the same time explaining why I didn't have them. I told the officer I left my purse on my desk at work.

His response was, "Sorry ma'am, I need you to step out of the car, please."

Because I couldn't produce the proper ID, I was escorted to the squad car. While in the back seat I felt a panic attack starting to come on. Tears started welling up in my eyes, and my heart was racing. When I looked up into his rear view mirror, I could see him staring at me. At that moment I felt I still had a chance of getting out of this mess. I sat up straight and composed myself.

After he finished running a check on my plates, he turned to look back at me. "I'm sorry Ms. Winters," he said. "I have to take you in for operating a vehicle without proper ID."

I was in total shock. All I could do was stare at him wide-eyed and open-mouthed. All of a sudden I burst out crying. I cried like a baby. All I could think was, my sisters will have a field day talking about me. I've tried to teach my son to always obey the law, and now look at me, sitting in a police car like a criminal. Oh God, I've never been in jail before. Well, it's no sense calling on God now. I'm going to be locked up with hookers and crack heads.

The officer didn't know what to do. I was becoming hysterical. Finally he calmed me down and informed me he was not going to arrest me. "Next time I will," he said. "You should always carry proper ID."

"I'll make sure it doesn't happen again, and thank you," I said, relieved.

Looking up into his face, I was certain I saw a smirk. "Are you laughing at me?" I asked. "Because this is no laughing matter." At that point I was getting angry. It's funny how your moods can change. "What is your name?" I demanded with authority.

"Officer McClean, ma'am," he answered. "And I wasn't making fun of you. It's just that you looked so innocent and cute. I wasn't going to arrest you. I only wanted to teach you a lesson. Someone else may not have been so kind. When I saw you falling apart, I knew I had gone too far."

"I was very afraid," I said. "You shouldn't do that to people."

"I'm sorry ma'am," he said. "Sometimes it's necessary in order to get people attention. And to help them understand the seriousness of what they've done. Can I make it up to you with dinner?"

Oh no you don't! I said to myself. The nerve of this man, asking me out on a date. This must be illegal!

"I don't think that would be a good idea," I told him as he escorted me back to my car. "I'm engaged to be married and it wouldn't be right.

"I understand," he said. Tipping his cap, he told me to have a good day and walked away.

I had lied about being engaged, and I would have loved having dinner with that fine man. But I remembered my friend who had dated a police officer. After she broke up with him, he stalked her for a week. And even had the nerve to give her a speeding ticket one evening, after following her. She couldn't do anything because she was in the wrong. All she wanted was that man out of her life, and not to stir up trouble. He eventually left her alone. I know that was one isolated case, and all cops are not like that kook. But it still made me leery about dating police officers.

I pulled off, leaving that fine man on the side of the road, not knowing I would run into him again two years later. By that time he had started his own private investigating service. I was definitely interested this time. Unfortunately for me, it was bad timing. I was relocating to Atlanta in six months.

Preston and I hit it off right away, and enjoyed each other immensely. A relationship was the last thing I was looking for. So I tried not to become involved, but to enjoy every moment we shared together. And they were few and far between. Making arrangements to move and helping my son get established and become independent for the first time, left little time for us.

But as the time to move grew closer, so did we. Very close, in fact. Preston decided to ride down with me to Atlanta. He wanted to help me get settled. I knew then that he was serious. That was the start of what we have today. A wonderful relationship built on friendship, and plenty of love.

Preston would fly to Atlanta every chance he could get. Our relationship became so serious, we decided to get married. I had to make a very difficult decision. To leave my job of 22 years and start over, or stay in Atlanta secure with a job, but miserable. I didn't want to start our marriage living in different states, having to commute to see each other. Long distance relationships or marriages rarely if ever work. But at that point in my life, I was ready to give up everything for stability. Especially in my personal life.

When I told Ashley, she freaked. "Why, Veronica?" she asked. "You're giving up 22 years. Jobs aren't easy to come by, especially making this kind of money. Think about what you're about to do, girl!"

I did think. Until I was mentally drained. Besides leaving my job, I was leaving my best friend. We'd been through a lot together in the 20 years of knowing each other.

When I finally made up my mind, I sat Ashley down and explained. I told her I felt like I was 18 years old again, unsure of where I belonged and what I was going to do with my life. But I was sure that I loved Preston and wanted to spend my life with him. And I definitely needed a change. I knew in my heart that if I was going to make a move, it had to be now. I really felt I would be moving forward and not backwards. And that I was getting ready to embark on a whole new career.

Looking at the sadness in her eyes, I wanted to hug her and say I wasn't going. But that was not to be. My mind was made up. So here I am, back in Michigan. I moved in with Preston and couldn't be happier, except for my status of being unemployed, and missing Ashley. Maybe I'll give her a call.

When Ronnie picks up the phone, there's no dial tone. "Hello," she says.

"I didn't hear the phone ring," the voice on the other end says.

"I guess not," Ronnie responds. "I picked up the phone before it could ring. I was going to call you! How ya doin' girlfriend?"

"Doing good," Ashley answers. "Guess who asked about you?"

"Who?"

"Jess. The girl who quit a month before you and moved to Nevada."

"Oh yeah," Ronnie says. "I remember her. How is she doing?"

"Really good. She's in town for her sister's wedding and decided to pay us a visit here in the office."

"If you see her again before she leaves, tell her I said hi. That is, if you can remember."

"Shut up silly girl, I'll remember," Ashley laughs. "Anyway, she couldn't believe you quit too. I told her, yeah chile, she moved back to be with that man of hers. And that you were getting married," she adds, laughing. "Don't worry, I didn't make you out to be a bimbo."

"I'm glad you didn't," Ronnie states. "I don't want her to think I was stupid and quit my job just to shack up."

"She also said congratulations." Before Ronnie can respond, Ashley continues. "I met a man today."

"Where?"

"You'll never guess."

"Why do you always want me to guess?" Ronnie asks. "You know I never do."

"Okay, you're right," she says. "I was on 285 when it happened." Ashley is so tickled, Ronnie has to wait until she finishes laughing to hear the rest. "Anyway," Ashley continues. "We were in this bad traffic jam, a little worse than the norm and at a standstill. I looked over at the car beside me. The man in the car was smiling, which seemed kinda' strange. But since I was bored, I smiled back and rolled down my window. He rolled down his, and it was on. We talked the whole time until traffic started moving along. I found out he worked for the news station, CNC. And his name is William Barkman. He's not really my type, but he looked okay. He also gave me his number. His home number, may I add."

"You go, girl," Ronnie says. "But a word of caution. Check this man out, because you don't know him. Maybe Preston can run a check on this guy."

"I'll think about it, MOM," she jokes. "Since I left your nest, I've been doing fine on my own."

"Okay, I get your point," Ronnie responds. "But the offer still stands."

"How is my buddy Preston?"

"Fine," Ronnie answers. "He's flying in today. As a matter of fact, he should be home in a couple of hours. So you know what that means."

"Yeah, yeah. It's time for me to get off my dime anyway. Try not to kill the man, and give me a call when you can."

"Okay, bye," Ronnie says.

After hanging up she thinks, I have just enough time to take a shower and finish getting things in order...

Ronnie is going to be really surprised, Preston thinks to himself. I love that woman. From the first time we met, although under unusual circumstances, I knew she was the one. I've never tried to pick up a woman while on duty. But I couldn't let her get away without trying. She's so loving and full of spirit. The sacrifices she's made to be with me are unbelievable. I've had women to go out of their way and do nice things, but Ronnie gave up her career. And switching my career was the best thing I've ever done.

I'd always wanted to be in law enforcement, so I became a cop. But it had some disadvantages. Police officers are stereotyped as bad husband material. I never had a problem getting women, but keeping them was a different ballgame.

Not too long after my first encounter with Ronnie, I met Gwen. We dated and eventually got married. But it was to be short-lived. We divorced after one year. After the divorce, I decided to start my own business. So I opened up a private investigator service. It turned out to be a good move. My personal life even got better. I began dating more often, and even had longer lasting relationships.

But none of the relationships were satisfying until I met Ronnie again. When she wanted me to meet her family, I knew she felt the same way I did. They're such a loving family. Something I'm not quite used to. I have no siblings, or should I say no family. Not in the traditional sense, anyway. I was raised by my grandmother, and she's no longer alive. She would have loved Ronnie and her family.

But Alex, my grandmother would have had to work on that one. That woman is so aloof. Not trusting of anyone. I was really surprised when Alex came over last week to see me and not Ronnie. And more surprised when she wanted to hire me. It seems Alex has her suspicions about Michael seeing another woman. So I took the case and flew to Chicago. Ronnie was not happy. We had plans that evening. All I could tell her was that I had to go out of town right away. I couldn't divulge any information, even if the client was her sister. Confidentiality is a must in this business. Since Michael was leaving for Chicago soon, it was imperative that I left immediately. Alex made sure I had all the information needed.

Now my job is done, and I'm ready to spend some quality time with my baby. I have a lot of making up to do.

"Aah, home at last," he says as he pulls into the parking lot. When he reaches the apartment door, he takes a deep breath, hoping Ronnie will forgive him for ruining their evening by leaving town so suddenly.

Upon entering their small but comfortable apartment, he stands there watching Ronnie take in the view of the lake. She isn't aware he's there.

"I love being home," she says out loud, looking out the window.

"And I love you," Preston says as he walks through the door. He drops his bags and walks towards her.

"Preston!" she says, startled. She swings around and smiles. "I'm so glad you're home."

"And who did I come home to?" he asks, smiling at her skimpy, sexy outfit.

"You like?" She twirls around. "My name is Venus. And you can have your way with me all night."

"All night?" he asks, nibbling on her neck. "I say let's get started."

"Oh no, not yet mister." She places her hand on his chest to stop him. "First I'm going to give you a champagne bath, and then oil you down. I want to please and then tease. After that, I'll watch you work your magic."

As Ronnie takes his hand to lead him down the hall, the door buzzer rings. "Noooo... Preston, don't push that button," she says, grabbing his arm. "They'll go away."

He looks at her, smiles, and continues down the hall to their destination.

The buzzer rings a second time. "Not again!" she yells. "Go away, you pest!"

Preston stops. "Ronnie, I'm sorry baby, but they're not going away. I'll see who it is and send them away. Okay, baby?"

"Alright, if you insist," she pouts.

While Preston heads towards the door, Ronnie goes to the bedroom. Waiting on Preston to get rid of whomever, she decides to move closer to the door and listen. That voice sounds familiar, she says to herself.

Opening the door just a little to take a peek, she sees Alex, visibly shaken, standing next to Preston. Taken aback at seeing Alex in such a fragile state, Ronnie runs out of the room to check on her sister. "Alex what's wrong?" she asks.

"Ronnie, let me sit down first to compose myself," Alex responds.

"Sure, I'm sorry," Ronnie says. "Come over here to the sofa."

After they're all seated, Ronnie asks again what's wrong. Alex is speechless. All she can do is stare at Ronnie.

"What's wrong?" Ronnie asks for the third time.

"Preston may love the way you're dressed," Alex says finally. "But that's not your hair, and I don't want to look at your breasts. Would you please go put on something presentable?"

Preston smiles, and Ronnie says, "I'm sorry, girl. I was so worried about you, I forget to get dressed. I'll run back into the bedroom and change."

While getting dressed Ronnie can hear whispering going on. She steps closer to the door to try and make out what's being said. All she can hear is Preston asking, "Why did you come here? We could have met tomorrow." Then Ronnie hears Alex apologize and say she's anxious, but her words starts to fade.

Ronnie flings open the door and walks into the room where they're sitting. "So what's up?" she asks, with her hands on her hips.

They both turn in unison, as if they were flat out busted. Preston speaks first. "What took you so long, baby?"

Ronnie totally ignores his question and turns her attention to Alex. "Are you here to see me, or Preston?"

"She's here to see me," Preston says.

Alex stands up and walks towards her. "Ronnie, I hired Preston," she says.

Ronnie's eyes widen in surprise. "You what? Why?"

"You know how miserable I've been," she answers. "I believe Michael is having an affair. So I hired Preston to follow him."

"Baby, that's why I went to Chicago," he says, now standing.

"This is unbelievable," Ronnie says.

"Look Ronnie," Alex pleads, "I didn't want you involved in this."

Ronnie looks away from Alex, feeling hurt.

"This is my business," Preston states. "And Alex is my client. I couldn't tell you what was going on."

"I know, Preston," Ronnie responds. "But this is my sister, for God sakes."

"This is all my fault," Alex says. "I shouldn't have come here. It wasn't the smartest thing to do. But you know how I am. I can get pretty persistant. I didn't mean to ruin your evening, I'm sorry."

"That's okay Alex," Ronnie says, walking over to give Alex a hug. "You're my sister, and I love you. Let's sit down and talk about it. It hurts me to see you so unhappy. I want to help if I can."

"I love you too," Alex responds. "But what I need right now, is to find out what's in that yellow envelope Preston's going to give me. I'm in limbo right now. Loving Michael hasn't been easy lately. But I do love him, and I want our marriage to work. What's in that envelope will determine our future."

"Ladies, I'm going to leave you two alone," Preston says, grabbing his bags. "I need to get that information for Alex."

After Preston leaves the room, Alex grabs Ronnie's hand. "I'm so afraid," she says. "Michael and I are so different. And he can be quite difficult at times. Putting up with his mother has been no picnic, either. I'd rather deal with all of that, though, than to have another failed marriage. But infidelity, I can't stomach."

"Listen girl," Ronnie says. "Whether those pictures prove infidelity or not, you two have issues. Talk to your husband. Communication is the key to resolving your issues. If he doesn't respond, well, at least you tried.

"Whatever those photos show, give him a chance to explain, and then make your decision. But if you decide to stay, make sure you've truly forgiven him. Everyone makes mistakes. If this is one too many for him, I say get him to stepping on out of there.

"Look, sweetie, I can talk on and on. But only you knows what goes on in your household. And if you feel your marriage can't be saved, then do what you must. I'm your sister. I'll be right there by your side, no matter what you decide.

"And I can't believe you allowed me to give you advice, without any interruptions," Ronnie finishes. At that they both laugh through teary eyes, then hug.

"Everything all right in here?" Preston asks as he walks back into the living room.

"We're fine baby," Ronnie says, wiping her eyes.

"I'm sorry it took so long, Alex," he says, handing over the envelope.

Alex nervously accepts the envelope and stares at it for a second. Then she looks up at Preston with questioning eyes. "Now that I have it, I'm afraid to open it," she says.

"You don't have to open it here," Ronnie comments. She places her hand on Alex's hand. "This is very personal, and I'm sure you'd rather do this in private. When is Michael coming home?"

"He took a later flight," Alex answers. "Around one in the morning, I think. And you're right, Ronnie. I need to do this in private."

As she stands up to leave she says, "Thank you Preston, for everything. I didn't mean to put you on the spot with Ronnie. And since you're part of the family, I'm sure it wasn't easy to spy on Michael."

"Don't worry about it," he says. "I'm a professional. And this is part of my job, like it or not. Although I will say, it was one of the hardest assignments I've ever had to do. Only because it was too close to home."

Ronnie moves over to Preston to put her arm around his waist, and he draws her close to him and kisses her forehead. "We're here for you if you need us," Ronnie says to her sister.

"Thanks, you two," Alex says, then walks out the door.

"I'm worried about her," Ronnie comments. "She loves Michael and really wants her marriage to work."

"What's to say it won't work?" Preston responds. "She needs to take a look at the information and decipher whether it's worth breaking up her marriage over." He smiles. "Let's say you go back into the bedroom, and come out looking like Venus."

Wiping tears from her eyes, Ronnie looks up at Preston. "Venus you want, Venus you'll get," she says.

He kisses her on the forehead, and whacks her on the butt as she turns and heads towards the bedroom.

On the drive home, Alex wonders what she's going to find out in the envelope sitting next to her. Will it end our marriage? she asks herself. Oh God, I don't believe I even did this. Hiring Preston to spy on my husband. I feel so guilty, but I was desperate. Maybe I should throw this envelope away, and put my trust in Michael. But if I do that, the question of infidelity will always remain in the back of my mind.

Goodness, I'm home already. Any other time it would take forever to get home. Because I dread opening up this envelope it made the drive seem shorter.

As Alex places the key into the lock, the door opens, startling her.

"Doris, you frightened me!" Alex says.

"I'm sorry ma'am," Doris responds. "I heard your car and didn't know whether you would need any assistance."

"No I don't, but thank you for inquiring."

"How was your evening out?" Doris asks.

"It was productive," she answers. "Did Mr. Crawford call?"

"No ma'am he didn't."

"I'm not surprised," she says, in a whisper.

"Ma'am?"

"Oh, I was talking to myself. That will be all, Doris."

"Yes ma'am."

"And Doris, hold all my calls, except for those from Mr. Crawford."

"Yes ma'am," Doris says, and walks away.

No sense in putting this off any longer, Alex says to herself. The only place I'll feel comfortable opening up this envelope is in my favorite room.

As she proceeds to go into the Glass Room, she stops to take in the smell of fresh flowers sitting on a table in the hallway. Once upon a time, she thinks, Michael would have flowers delivered to me just because. I felt so special. Now he makes me feel as if I'm a piece of the furniture. Something to use when he's here. Enough of this daydreaming. It's time to come back to reality and get down to business.

Alex holds the envelope close to her chest and head towards the Glass Room. After entering the room she closes the door for privacy. "Now," she says out loud as she flops down onto the sofa. "Let's see what Michael's been up to."

Just as she starts to open the envelope there's a knock on the door.

"Yes, Doris!" Alex calls out.

"Excuse me ma'am," Doris responds as she enters the room. "I'm sorry to disturb you, but I thought you could use a cocktail. Also, Mrs. Findley called, inquiring about dinner tomorrow night."

"Thank you Doris, I really do need this drink right now."

"Is there anything else I can get you?"

"No, that will be all."

As Doris leaves the room, Alex recalls the last maid they had. What was her name? she asks herself. Oh yes, Trixey. How could I forget. She thought she was going to show my husband some tricks. But I had news for her. I'm the woman of this house. No tricks are done in this house with my husband unless it's by me. I fired her, then threw her butt out! Doris, on the other hand, is wonderful. Plus she's too old to throw her legs up for Michael. She probably knows a lot of tricks, but she's too old to use them. Anyway, back to the envelope. No, that can wait. I better call Paris back first.

Alex stares at the envelope, then rubs her hand over it. "I pray you've been faithful, Michael," she says out loud. She then picks up the phone and calls Paris.

It rings several times. "No answer," Alex says. "Maybe she stepped out. I'll leave a message."

"Hello," says the voice on the other end.

"Hey Paris," Alex says. "I thought you were out, so I was going to leave a message. Are you busy?"

"No I'm not," Paris says. "I've been letting the answering machine pick up the calls. Someone's been calling and hanging up. Some woman called before you, asking if I can trust my husband."

"Did you tell Neil about it?"

"No, not yet. But I will. Anyway, can you make dinner tomorrow?"

"Sure can," Alex answers. "I'm looking forward to it."

"Then I'll see you tomorrow."

"Okay, talk to you then."

After hanging up the phone, Alex picks up the envelope. "I've put this off long enough," she announces out loud.

She takes a deep breath and proceeds to open the envelope. She pulls out the photos slowly, looking at each one as if she was a jeweler appraising a stone.

59

Before she can finish, she stands up, letting the photos fall to the floor, and steps on them as she makes her way to the bar.

"Get back in this bed, woman, and let the machine get that call."

"No, Preston," Ronnie says. "It might be Alex calling. Let me go!"

"Come to Big Daddy," he says, holding her back.

Screaming and kicking, Ronnie reaches for the phone. "Hello," she answers.

"Did I pick the wrong time to call?" Paris asks.

"Hey Paris," Ronnie says, laughing. "What's up?"

"This is a quick call about dinner. Can you make it tomorrow?"

"I think I can. What time?"

"Is 6 o'clock okay with you?"

"Yep."

"Then 6 o'clock it is," Paris says. "I called Alex and she's coming too. So is Les."

"Where are we going, so I can dress appropriately?"

"I'll call you after Les and I check out her new building," Paris answers.

"Okay, talk to you tomorrow," Ronnie says as she hangs up the phone.

"Come here, woman," Preston smiles, pulling Ronnie over to him.

"You are so bad, Preston. But I love it."

"So what's with the dinner plans? Am I invited, or is it girl's night out?"

"Girl's night out, baby. We can't talk about you guys if you're there."

"That's because you all are cowards," he comments.

"We're really doing you a favor."

"How so?"

"By sparing you pain," she laughs.

"I'm going to show you pain," he says, grabbing and tickling her. "Now say 'I'm a coward,' over and over."

Finally she gives in. "I'm a coward! I'm a coward!" she gasps, tears of laughter rolling down her face.

He pulls her to him and holds her tight, then kisses her tenderly. "I love you Ronnie."

"I love you too," she says with passion. "You make me feel so special when I'm with you. I don't see myself as a useless and unproductive person."

"You are special," he says lovingly. "I understand why you feel this way, however you must remain positive. The jobs you interviewed for, were not for you. And there's a good reason why you didn't get them."

"And why is that, Big Daddy?"

"Because the right one is waiting for you."

"Well, I'll be glad when the right one comes along," she comments dryly.

"I think it has," he says. "A friend of mine has a position open. It would be perfect for you."

"Really!" she says, excited. "Call your friend, get the information so I can check it out."

"Better yet," he responds, "why don't I call him now and see if we can swing by?"

"Preston, it's late."

"I'm sure he wouldn't mind. Now go ahead and start the shower. I'm right behind you."

As Ronnie heads towards the bathroom, Preston calls his friend. "Matt, this is Preston. What's going on, man?"

"Business as usual, man," Matt says. "Still spying on folks?"

"Only if I have a reason to."

"I may need to use your services," Matt says. "I'm just not sure if I can afford you."

"You can afford me alright," Preston responds. "You're rolling in dough."

"So what's up?"

"I need to get things rolling on what we discussed."

"Cool with me. Just give me a date and time."

"How about tonight? Let's say, in a couple of hours. We can meet at your favorite spot."

"That will work," Matt answers. "I'll check you out later, man. Got to make a quick run."

"Oh, something else man," Preston says. "I'm bringing my lady with me."

"So I'll get a chance to meet the beautiful Veronica," Matt says. "That's cool. I'll bring my friend too."

"Okay, later man," Preston responds. "Tonight should be quite interesting," he says as he heads towards the bathroom to join Ronnie.

After they shower and dress Ronnie repeatedly asks questions about the job. But Preston doesn't give in. She tries all the way to their destination, but to no avail.

When Preston pulls into a parking lot where a boat was docked, Ronnie becomes quiet. "Preston, baby, why are we here? I thought we were going to your friend Matthew's house."

"Well baby, I felt a different atmosphere would make you feel more comfortable and relaxed," he answers. "With that combination, you can work your magic on my man. Besides, I think we both worked up quite an appetite, don't you?"

"Ummm, yes we did. And when we get home, we're going to work our dinner off."

"I'm always game for that," he says with a mischievous smile. "Are you ready to meet the man who's going to start your new career?"

"Yep, let's go."

As they enter the dinner boat, they're greeted by a very handsome man. "Glad you made it, man," he says, shaking Preston's hand.

"I'm a man of my word," Preston responds. "Matthew, I'd like you to meet Veronica Winters. Veronica, this is Matthew."

"It's a pleasure to meet you," Ronnie says, extending her hand.

"No, it's my pleasure," he responds with a grin as wide as the Detroit River. Such a beautiful smile and perfectly white teeth, Ronnie says to herself.

"I've heard so much about you Veronica," he says. "You're even more beautiful than Preston described."

"Why thank you," she says, looking over at Preston as he winks. "Please go on, tell me more."

"All I have to say is that my buddy over here didn't do you justice," Matthew says.

"Is that so," she responds.

"Okay, that's enough," Preston says. "Down boy."

They all laugh and head towards their table. "If you two will excuse me," Matthews says, "I'm going to find my date."

"Preston," Ronnie says, "you didn't tell me this was a double date. I thought we're here to discuss business."

"We are baby. But there's nothing wrong with mixing business with a little pleasure."

"You're right. I'm afraid I might forget about business in this place. It's so beautiful and romantic."

Looking out into the Detroit River at night, with the water reflecting the lights and the sound of jazz in the background, sends Ronnie into a daze. She wishes this moment would last forever.

"Baby, wake up," Preston whispers. "The waiter is here. Do you want a drink?"

"Yes," she says, snapping out of her beautiful dream.

"Chardonnay please, and for me Martell," Preston tells the waiter.

When the waiter returns with their drinks he also has a bottle of champagne. "Excuse me sir," Ronnie says. "We didn't order the champagne."

"The gentleman did, ma'am," he answers. "Is there anything else I can get for you?"

"No, that will be all, thank you," Preston answers.

"What is the champagne for, you sneak?" Ronnie asks.

"To celebrate your new beginning," he answers, with a mischievous smile.

"I don't know what that smile is all about, but it seems as if you know something I don't."

He leans over and gives her a kiss on the cheek. "All I know is that all your dreams are about to come true," he says with a smile.

As Ronnie is about to sip her wine, she spots Matthew walking towards the table with a man. "Preston," she whispers, "I thought Matthew was going to find his date."

"That is his date," Preston says. "Matthew is gay."

"But he looks as straight as a board."

"You don't need a certain look to be gay," he answers.

"Well his friend has the look," she says. "He struts more than I do."

"Behave yourself, Ronnie. I know how you are when you get a little wine in you."

"Don't worry," she says, smiling. "I won't embarrass you." Then she nudges him.

"Preston, Veronica," Matthew says. "I'd like you to meet my significant other. This is Clay."

"Good meeting you, man," Preston says.

"That's not a man," Ronnie whispers to Preston.

"He is a man," he whispers back. "His sexual preference is different, that's all."

"Yes, nice meeting you," Ronnie finally says with a stutter. "And you can call me Ronnie."

"Okay," Clay says, with a high-pitched voice and a smile. "So I see you two started without us. Bad kids," he says, tapping Ronnie lightly on the arm.

"Why yes, I'm afraid we did," Ronnie answers, embarrassed.

"Clay," Matthew speaks up. "Why don't you go and get our drinks."

"Why of course, darling," Clay answers. "Excuse me everyone. I'll return shortly." He heads towards the bar, strutting his stuff.

Preston has to clear his throat to get Matthew's full attention.

"Oh, I'm sorry guys," Matthew says. "Clay is a showoff, and I love it. He loves using terms of endearment. Sometimes I wonder if he knows my real name. We've been dating about six months now. He's really a sweetheart, and a very smart man. And he's the one, Ronnie my dear, who you must impress."

"What line of work is he in?" she asks.

"Clay owns a clothing store," Matthew answers. "He's flying to New York in the morning to open a second store. That's where you come in, my dear. He needs someone to operate the store he has in the New Center area."

"I'm back, and here's your drink, darling," Clay says. "Now, Miss Veronica. I'm sorry, you want to be called Ronnie," he says, gesturing with his hand. "Well Miss Ronnie, I'm sure this handsome man of mine filled you in on my business, and the position I have available."

"Yes he did," she answers. "And it sounds wonderful. I'm definitely interested in hearing more about the position."

"I'm flying out first thing in the morning," he says. "Here's my card. Give my secretary a call and she'll set up an appointment for us to talk further.

"Well folks," he says after downing his drink, "it's been a pleasure, but I must bid you good night. And Ronnie, make that appointment, sugar."

"Trust me, I will," she responds. "And have a safe trip."

"Yell man, have a safe trip," Preston says.

Clay gives Preston a look as if he's offended, then turns his attention to Matthew.

"See, I told you," Ronnie whispers. "He doesn't even consider himself a man."

"Hush," Preston whispers back.

"You don't have to whisper," Matthew remarks. "You two can talk more freely when I walk Clay out."

As he attempts to stand, Clay places a hand on his shoulder. "Don't bother," Clay says. "I can find my way out. Anyway, I'll see you later," he says with a wink, and then walks away.

"I want to thank you, Matthew, for all you've done," Ronnie says.

"No problem," he responds. "Now I'm going to give you two some privacy."

"You don't have to leave," she says.

"Yes he does," Preston responds.

"Preston, don't be rude," Ronnie says sweetly.

"No big deal," Matthew says. "Preston and I go back a long way. He's like my brother. Preston, take care, man. I'm going to get another drink, then I'm outta here."

"Okay man. Thanks for helping my lady."

"That's what friends are for. Enjoy your evening, and good night," he says, and walks away.

"Oh Preston, let's open the champagne," Ronnie says excitedly.

"Why don't we order first, I'm starved." He signals the waiter and places their order. After the waiter returns with their food, Ronnie is so excited she can't eat any more than her salad. "Thank you so much for such a lovely evening," she says.

"Don't thank me yet," Preston answers as he finishes his meal. "The night isn't over yet. Just listen to this next song."

Ronnie stares at him with a puzzled look. All of a sudden the band stops playing and the deejay takes over. "This next song is for a very special lady," he says. "This is for Veronica."

The music starts. "I love that song," Ronnie says in a high pitched tone. "How did he know? You didn't even leave your seat."

"Matthew did me the favor," Preston smiles.

"You sneak," she says. "Let's dance."

"Why don't we sit here and enjoy the music?"

That's strange, she thinks to herself. Preston loves to dance. And the deejay is playing *This Is My Promise*, by the Temptations. It's our favorite song.

While looking at Preston with a puzzled look, Ronnie starts moving in her chair, to the beat of the music. "That's the perfect wedding song," she comments, still trying to entice Preston onto the dance floor. "Especially the part that says, 'Will You Marry Me.'"

Preston still didn't make a move, but smiles to himself as he watches her body sway.

As soon as the music gets to the part of the song Ronnie had mentioned, it stops.

"Why did the deejay stop the music?" she questions. Noticing the sudden brightness, she realizes the spotlight is shining on them. "Preston, why is the spotlight on us and no one else?" she asks nervously.

Preston turns to face Ronnie, taking her hand into his. "I love you Ronnie," he expresses with sincerity. "I want to make this official. Will you marry me?"

All Ronnie can do is look at him wide-eyed, with her hand over her mouth. Preston pulls out a small velvet box and opens it. There sits a beautiful 3-carat diamond ring. Ronnie gasps and becomes totally speechless. Finally she says, with tears in her eyes, "Oh yes, I'll marry you."

Preston slowly removes the ring and gently slips it on her slender finger. He kisses her hand, then passionately kisses her on the lips.

Everyone in the room starts clapping, and the deejay starts the song over. Preston leads Ronnie onto the dance floor. Gazing into her eyes, he proclaims his love.

"I will cherish you, protect you, and love you always," he says, while holding her close. "This is my promise to you, Veronica Winters."

"And I'm going to make this a night for you to remember," she says back lovingly.

They stop dancing, look at each other, then walk off the floor and out the door.

Belinda Walker-Graham

CHAPTER FIVE

"That was sooo good sweetheart. I relish these moments with you," she says. "Between your job, my business, and the twins, we never spend enough quality time together."

"I know, honey," Neil responds. "But I sure do miss the boys when they're away."

"Your mother is bringing them home tomorrow," Paris comments. "I say treasure the moment."

"Well then, instead of going out to dinner, let's nibble on each other," he says.

"You're speaking my language. However I think we need to eat something that will give us energy. We've burnt quite a bit already."

"One wouldn't think so, the way you're rubbing your feet up and down my legs."

Laughing, she slides her hand down until it reaches its destination. Food becomes a distant memory.

Afterwards, Paris lies awake in her husband's arms while he sleeps, remembering how close they had come to ending it all.

Around the time the twins turned nine, she says to herself, Neil suddenly wanted to go back into his early adult years. After surviving the seven year itch, I thought we were home free. But to my surprise it happened two years behind schedule. I tried to block it out of my mind and pretend this wasn't happening to us. I convinced myself it was all the stress Neil was under. With a shortage of pilots, he was working overtime, which meant he was never at home. I was raising the boys all alone and trying to start my own business. It became unbearable. We no longer were one, but individuals leading separate lives. Intimacy no longer existed between us.

Then the deception came. After that, I no longer wanted to continue the charade. I figured I could be miserable alone. So we separated. Even though we both agreed that was the only solution, I still wanted an explanation. I never got one. He did not try to explain the affair, or say he was sorry. He was only sorry he got caught. It's funny how different men and women are when it comes to affairs. Women are more discrete, whereas men are very careless. I'm still trying to figure that one out. I don't know if they want to get caught, or they're just plain stupid. Either way, it boils down to whatever you do in the dark, always come to light.

After I got into my routine without Neil in my life, I started dating so I wouldn't dwell on my problems. To me that's wasted energy. And I need all my energy for the boys, and my new endeavor. Dating was a diversion for me. And Leonard was just what the doctor ordered. I met him at Rico's Place, a club that feature new talents on Wednesday nights. And most of the amateurs were rap artists. Rap is okay, but not my thing. Give me some old-school music or jazz, and I'm yours for the taking. But when a co-worker asked if I wanted to go, I said yes. I thought it would be fun, and most definitely different.

And fun it was. I had a blast. One would have thought I was 25 years old. I sure thought so, and I proved it by hooking up with one. Leonard was so cute. He had such a sparkling smile, and that wasn't due to white teeth. More like gold. I thought to myself, that's okay, he's from the south. We can work on that. After all, that's what a dentist is for.

To my surprise, he wasn't from the south. He told me this was his own unique style as a rap artist. Not unique, I thought, but who cared? I was only in it for the fun. He told me he was trying to cut a CD. So in other words he was broke. And he drove an awful old ugly car. The first time I tried to get in that car, the door wouldn't open. I said to myself, Oh no, he won't get me trapped in this car and rape me, or worse. After all I really didn't know anything about him. From that point on, I drove my BMW. But I have to admit, Leonard was a lot of fun, and a good lay. I needed both.

After a while I started getting bored and wanted my old life back. Neil must have felt the same way because he started coming around. His excuse at the beginning was to see the boys. As time went on, we started getting close and decided to make a go of it again. I guess he realized the grass is not always greener on the other side.

"Hey you," Neil says as he reaches over and pulls her closer.

"I thought you were sleeping," she responds with a smile.

"I was for a minute," he answers. "But when I looked over at my beautiful wife, I couldn't close my eyes again. I rarely see you with your hair loose. But you looked so intense. What were you thinking about?"

"How happy I am we're back together," she answers. "We almost blew it, you know," she says softly.

"Paris, let's put the past behind us. I was a fool, and didn't realize what I was losing. But now I do. All that foolishness is over. I would never jeopardize what we have again. You and the boys mean the world to me. Now let's look forward, not backwards. We have a wonderful future ahead of us."

"That's just what I'm going to do," she says. "I'm going to look forward. Starting right now, by getting up and taking a shower." She gives him a smack on the lips and jumps out of bed.

While taking a shower, she can barely hear what Neil is saying. As she enters the bedroom she says, "Now start over sweetheart, I couldn't hear a word you were saying to me." Walking over to the bed and wrapping a towel around her head, she flops down. "All I could hear was something Preston, and Michael."

"Okay, I'll start over," he says as he takes the lotion to rub her down. "Remember earlier this week when I had to fly to Chicago two days in a row?"

"How could I forget. I was so happy you were scheduled on short flights both days."

"Well, it was so ironic. The first day Preston was on my flight, and the next day I saw Michael boarding."

"Alex told me Michael was taking a business trip to Chicago," she says. "Ronnie never mentioned Preston going to Chicago. But then again, due to the nature of Preston's work, she might not have known. He tries not to involve Ronnie. Anyway, it was probably a coincidence."

"I'm sure it was," he responds, rubbing her thighs.

74

"I think this is getting good to you," she comments, as she watched his hands move higher. "Sweetheart, why don't you shower and then run out to get us a bite to eat. I'm ravished."

"I thought you wanted to eat out," he responds.

"I changed my mind, sweetheart," she says, then winks. "Besides, I want to spend some quality time with my man."

Smiling, Neil jumps up and runs to the bathroom. Paris throws back her head and starts laughing.

While getting dressed, she starts thinking how strange that Preston and Michael ended up in the same place. That Alex, she says to herself. You little sneak. You hired Preston after all.

She doesn't hear Neil walk up behind her, and he startles her. Turning around, she smacks him on the arm. "You could get hurt that way, mister," she says through clenched teeth.

Smiling, he grabs her. "And what could you do to hurt me?" he asks while swinging her around.

"Stop it Neil," she says, laughing. "Get dressed and get me something to eat before I eat you."

"Mmmmm, that sounds good," he says. Paris pushes him away and starts pouting.

"Okay, you big baby," he says while starting to get dressed. "How 'bout a pizza?"

"I don't care what you get. As long as it's edible. I'll even call and order."

After getting dressed, Neil heads downstairs, with Paris on his heels. As soon as he reaches the bottom step he turns quickly, knocking Paris a little off balance. "Now give me something to come back home to," he says.

Paris plants a wet one on him. "How was that?" she asks. All he can do is moan and hurry out the door.

Walking towards the kitchen, Paris starts thinking about Alex. I wonder if Ronnie know what's going on? Probably not, due to client confidentiality. Preston would never divulge any information regarding his clients. I think I'll give Miss Alex a call. She can't keep a secret for long, even if it's her own. She'll burst.

On her way to the phone, Paris stops to pick up the family photo, and smiles. I miss my boys, she says to herself. When times were hard for me emotionally, they always brought a smile to my face. They'd argue about who was the man of the house. Protecting me was their mission in life. For a while, I had to be mother and father, which gave me insight on single parenthood. I take my hat off to all the single parents, whether it's the mother or father, going at it alone. Between basketball practice, PTA meetings, and my job, I was whipped. That's why I jumped at the opportunity to go to that club with my co-workers. I needed an outlet. Keeping Leonard around relieved my stress.

Shaking off the memories, Paris picks up the phone to call Alex. To her surprise, there's no answer. When the machine comes on she leaves a message. "Hey sis, Paris. Call me."

Wow, she says to herself, Alex out and about. Good for her. She needs to do other things besides sitting by the phone waiting for that husband of hers to call. And where is my husband? I'm starved. If he doesn't hurry up, I'm going to pass out. I'll give Les a call to pass the time away. I know she's home.

Probably working on some figures to get her shop up and running.

After the second ring, Paris begins to get irritated. "I can't seem to catch anyone at home," she says out loud. "Well, I won't leave a message, I'll just hang up."

Before she can, a voice comes on the other end. "Hello," Les says, out of breath.

"I didn't think anyone was home," Paris comments. "What were you doing? You sound as if you ran to the phone."

"I did," Les answers. "I was upstairs picking out a suit for our meeting with Mr. Langley tomorrow."

"Oh Les, I totally forgot about the meeting. Around noon, right?"

"Yes Paris, and do I need to remind you tomorrow?"

"No, Miss Thang, I'm sure I wrote it in my planner, but I'll check."

"Good, because this is important to me," Les responds. "I really need you there."

"Don't worry, I'll be there," Paris sings.

"Please don't try to sing," Les says, laughing. "Your voice is worse than ever. You never could hold a note, and you have the worse voice in the family."

"I don't think so," Paris replies. "I think Ronnie does."

"I forgot," Les agrees, "Ronnie does sound pretty bad. I sure hope she's not at home serenading Preston."

"Come on now, Les. You know Ronnie. She's too busy being Freaky to sing."

By now Les is laughing so hard tears are running down her cheeks. "Wipe your face Les," Paris says,

77

knowing what was happening. "You always get carried away when you laugh."

"Girl, I needed that. All I've been thinking about is the meeting tomorrow with Mr. Langley. I'm a nervous wreck."

"Girl, you'll do just fine," Paris says. "How is my brother-in-law doing?"

"Who?"

"What do you mean, who?" Paris responds. "My brother-in-law. Steve, your husband."

"Oh, he's fine," she answers in a dry tone. "And how's Neil?"

"He's great, or should I say we're doing great. He went out for pizza. I expected him home by now. It doesn't take that long. I called ahead of time and the place is only five minutes away."

"Slow down girl," Les says. He's probably on his way home."

Listening to smooth jazz while waiting on the pizza, Neil gets a page. I bet it's Paris wondering what's taking so long, he says to himself. Poor baby. She sure worked up an appetite, he thinks, smiling.

Checking the number on his pager brings a puzzled look to his face. He doesn't recognize it. He picks up his cell phone and calls the number.

"Hello," says the familiar voice on the other end.

"Did someone page?" he asks, puzzled.

"Hey sugar, it me."

"Marlene!" he says, surprised. "Why are you paging me, and what do you want? Wait a minute. Are you here in Michigan?"

"Slow down sugar," she responds. "I can only answer one question at a time. To answer your first question. I want to see you, that's why I paged. And second, yes I am in Michigan. Aren't you happy?"

"I suppose you conveniently forgot our last conversation," he answers. "What we had was over a long time ago. I love my wife, and you and I could never rekindle what we had."

"Neil, I know you only went back to Paris because of the boys. You love me, not her. Those were your words, not mine."

"That was during the time I was confused," he answers. "You were only a diversion, Marlene. It was fun while it lasted, but now it's over. You hear me?" he says angrily. "Over!" he yells, then turns off the cell phone.

Not surprised with Neil's reaction, Marlene gently puts down the phone with a smile. "He'll come around," she says, staring at their picture. "He loves me. That bitch Paris. She's using those boys to hold on to him."

Marlene then puts the picture down and starts to file her nails. "Well, we will see who wins in the end, Miss Bitch," she says while staring at a nail, not noticing the blood.

While driving home Neil reflects on his affair with Marlene. How could I be so stupid? he asks himself. To get involved with such a nut case. The wrong I've done is now coming back to haunt me. How am I going to get out of this mess? he wonders, rubbing his close-cropped head. The woman is relentless. She'll stop at nothing to destroy my marriage. I can't let that happen. Paris cannot be hurt a second time.

Pulling into the drive, he suddenly thinks about how worried Paris must be. "I've been gone a long time," he says.

Neil hurries out of the car with pizza in hand, thinking of an explanation to give Paris. Walking through the door, he notices Paris pacing.

Hearing the door shut, Paris makes a sudden turn. "Thank God you're home, Neil. I was beginning to get worried."

"I'm sorry, honey," he says as he walks over to give her a hug.

"You should have at least called to let me know you were okay."

"I only went to get a pizza, Paris. You're calmer when I'm flying the plane."

"At least I know where you are," she says, starting to get irritated.

"What's that supposed to mean?" he asks sharply. "You don't trust me?"

"You've given me plenty of reasons not to," she snaps back.

"So we're back to that again? I thought we put that behind us, Paris. But I guess I'm the only one who did."

"Oh Neil, I'm sorry," she says, walking over to put her arms around him. Stepping back, Neil looks at her and shakes his head. "I think I'll skip the pizza and go on up to bed," he says. "I have an early flight anyway."

Paris, not moving, looks through teary eyes as Neil leaves to go upstairs. Walking over to the pizza box, she realizes she isn't hungry either. Her appetite had been ruined.

When she touches the pizza box, she feels how cold the box is.

Neil's been somewhere else besides the pizza place, she says to herself. Why else would it be so cold? No, I won't do this. I will not allow my mind to run wild with crazy thoughts. I will not let that woman destroy my marriage a second time. But why can't I forget the past? Have I truly forgiven my husband? I thought I had. Enough time has gone by.

"Stop it, Paris," she says out loud. "What I need to do is go and apologize to my husband." She turns to go upstairs.

At that very moment, Marlene says, "I owe that bitch anyway. Neil and I were doing just fine until she showed her ass in Houston. The nerve of her, following him like that."

Marlene begins to reminisce.

What a good thing Neil and I had. We met on a flight from Detroit to Houston. I was the last passenger off the plane. While I was looking around for my ride, out walked the pilot. He was too fine. Very tall, like a basketball player. I said to myself, I must meet that brother. It's very rare to see a black pilot. So I'm thinking, he must have it going on.

I started walking in his direction, looking around as if in search of someone. Then I conveniently bumped into him, and released my bags onto the floor purposely, although he thought I dropped them.

"Excuse me," he said. "I'm so sorry."

Belinda Walker-Graham

"It's not your fault," I responded. "I bumped into you, not watching where I was going. My name is Marlene." Then I extended my hand.

"I'm Neil," he said back, taking my hand to shake it. "Well Miss Marlene, let me pick up your bags for you."

I noticed how he looked at my legs while gathering my bags. Oh yes, Mr. Pilot man, I said to myself, I see you checking out my long legs. Right then and there, I knew he was interested. But would he act on it? I needed to find out more about him.

"Thank you for being such a gentlemen," I said.

"You're welcome," he answered. "Anything for such an attractive woman."

"With such a compliment, and of course a good deed, you should be rewarded. Why not join me for a drink?"

"A drink sounds a bit too much for me right now. But I will take you up on a cup of coffee."

We went to a little coffee shop in the airport, where most of the pilots and attendants frequent. In the midst of talking and laughing we were interrupted by another pilot.

"Hey Neil. Thought you were at the hotel by now, since you were so tired."

"I think exhausted is the word for it, Paul. It's been a long day. Oh, forgive me, Marlene. This is my co-pilot Paul. And Paul, this is Marlene."

"Hello Marlene, nice to meet you," he said.

"Same," I replied, not at all happy to be interrupted.

"Well, I'm outta here buddy," Paul said. "Gotta call the wife. Tell Paris and the boys hi when you talk

82

to her," he said, while looking at me. "Nice meeting you Marlene."

I smiled and nodded. Asshole, I said to myself, then turned my attention back to Neil.

"So you have a family?" I asked.

"If you want to know if I'm married, yes I am," he answered. "Are you?"

"No. I see you don't pull any punches, Neil."

"I'm sorry, but I'm exhausted. I apologize for being so brash."

"Apology accepted," I said with a smile.

"Let's start over tomorrow with dinner," he said.

I smiled and handed him a piece of paper. "Call me," I said. Then I stood up and left. That was the beginning.

The next day Neil called. It was a wonderful evening. We talked about his marriage, and his dreams of becoming a pilot. He also made it clear that companionship was all he wanted out of our affair. When he's in town, we can hook up, but leaving his family was not an option. I accepted that.

The day that bitch caught us, I was planning a wonderful evening. I had just left the beauty shop from having my braids redone. Just as I turned the engine off, I noticed a cab pull up behind me. I smiled with anticipation, then jumped out and ran to greet my lover. Before I knew it, Neil was crunched over in pain. I was holding my head and looking at my braids laying on the ground. When I looked up finally, that bitch had made it to the cab. She was actually looking out the window and giving us the finger as the cab pulled off.

Needless to say, the night was ruined, along with our good thing. Neil was not the same after that. Our lovemaking was not as intense. Oh, we still saw each other from time to time. His body was here, but his mind was in Michigan.

Then one day out of the blue, Neil appeared at my door without calling. I could tell by the look on his face, and his evasive manner, what he was about to say. And I was right. It was over.

I begged and begged, but to no avail. I even lied and told him I might be pregnant, to keep him around. He was shaken at first, but then composed himself. "It doesn't matter whether you're pregnant or not Marlene," he said. "It's still over. If it's true, I will take care of the baby. But I want nothing else to do with you romantically."

"Get out," I spat, then slapped him. He left with the door hitting his back.

I couldn't believe he was going back to that woman to work on his marriage. I loved Neil, and deep down inside I knew he loved me. He was just fighting it, that's all. And feeling obligated because of the boys.

I have to make him realize it's me he loves and needs. Anyway, she's so stupid. I've been calling and saying nasty things, then hanging up. I need to make her suspicious of Neil. And when she throws him out, I'll be waiting with open arms. Maybe I should just speed up the process.

Marlene walks over to the phone and punches in Neil's home number.

"Hello," Neil says.

No answer. Neil hangs up the phone. I can bet it was Marlene, he says to himself. Now, how did she get my home number? I have to do something about her.

Hoping the phone didn't wake Paris, he looks over and notices the bed empty. I could have swore I heard Paris come upstairs, he thinks.

Neil goes downstairs to find Paris asleep on the chaise lounge in the family room, with a book on her chest. "My beautiful Paris," he says. "I know we took vows for better or worse. But why are we always experiencing the worse? This time around, it's all on me. I bear the burden, and I'm going to lift it. I've got to make things right again," he says, turning to go back upstairs.

He doesn't know Paris was listening.

I shouldn't have spoken those words to him, she thinks. He's really hurting. Maybe I should heat up the pizza and take some upstairs to him. We've had such a wonderful day, and I don't want to end it fighting.

While Paris is waiting on the pizza to heat, the phone rings again.

"Hello," Paris says.

No response.

"Hello," she says again.

"I'm sorry," the woman says on the other end. "I must have the wrong number." Then she hangs up.

Paris looks at the caller ID. It shows 'private.'

This is happening too many times, she thinks. First I get hang ups. Then cursed at. Now this. I wonder if it's the same woman who called me a bitch? The voice sounds the same. What's going on? I don't want to think Neil is at it again. But how can I not? He did it once, that I know of. I need to handle this delicately. I

85

don't want to falsely accuse him. But on the other hand, he's not going to make a fool out of me twice.

The beep of the microwave interrupts her train of thought. Then the phone rings again. "Hello," she answers, cautiously.

"Hi mom."

"Hey Brian," she responds happily.

"I'm on the phone too," another voice says.

"I'm sorry Brandon," she says. "I should have known you were on the phone too. Hi, my babies. Wait a minute. What are you two doing up at this time of night?"

"Grandma said we could call you if we make it quick," Brian says. "We miss you and dad."

"Well, we miss both of you too," she says lovingly.

"When are we coming home?" Brandon asks.

"I'll pick you guys up tomorrow after school."

"All right!" they both say in unison.

"Now don't sound so happy," she says. "We don't want to make Grandma feel bad, okay boys?"

"Ok mom," they said. "Where's dad? We want to talk to him too."

"Sorry guys, your dad is sleeping. I'll make sure he calls tomorrow. Now, I think it's time for you guys to call it a night. You have school tomorrow."

"Ok mom," they said. "Don't forget to tell dad to call us."

"I will, my babies. Did you boys have homework today?"

"Yes, and Grandma tried to help us," Brian says.

"She didn't understand what we were supposed to do. So she threw up her hands and left the room shaking her head," Brandon says laughing.

"Well Brandon, Grandma is much older, and it's been a long time since she was in school. A lot has changed since then. I hope you boys didn't make her feel bad."

"Oh no mom," Brian said. "We love Grandma. We wouldn't do that."

"I know you wouldn't do that purposely," she says kindly. "And I know how much you two love your Grandma. Tell her I said hi, and I'll see her tomorrow, okay guys?"

"Okay, mom. We love you," they both said.

"And I love the both of you. Good night, my loves."

After hanging up, Paris turns to see Neil walking into the kitchen. "Did I hear the phone ring?" he asks.

"Yes you did. Our babies called."

"Sweetheart, they're not babies anymore."

"They're my babies, no matter how old they get," she responds. "And before I forget, make sure you call them tomorrow. They want to talk to their daddy."

"I most certainly will," he answers as he grabs her around the waist and pulls her close. "I'm sorry sweetheart for the way I behaved earlier. It was uncalled for. Especially after the wonderful day we had."

"Baby, you were reading my mind. I'm sorry too, Neil. I heated the pizza."

"Good," he says. "I was wondering when you were going to feed me."

"I'm going to feed you, alright," she responds excitedly. "Food to mouth resuscitation is what I call it."

"Is that right?"

"Yep. I'm going to bring back your stamina and wear you out all over again."

"I take back what I said earlier," he responds.

"And what's that?"

"How I miss the boys when they're not here. I'm so glad they're with my mother," he says, nibbling on her ear.

"Hold it, cowboy," she says, pulling away. "Let's eat first, then I'll show you how I can ride."

"Ok, let's eat and have good conversation," he says with a wink.

They sit down to eat and he continues, "So when are you picking up the boys?"

"Tomorrow after school. I thought it would be good for your mom to have them around a little while longer. She enjoys them so much."

"I know she does," he says sadly. "Since dad passed away, she's very lonely in that big house. And living so close to us makes her feel safe. We can check on her, and the boys can visit her after school lets out."

"Changing the subject a bit sweetheart," she interrupts, "did I hear the phone ring earlier, or was I dreaming?"

"I was hoping it didn't wake you," he answers. "It did ring, but no one was on the other end. I guess they had the wrong number."

"I knew I heard the phone ring." She thinks, this is the perfect time to bring up the other calls. Nah, I think not. Why should I spoil my night? I'll deal with the mystery woman another day. "Ready to go for a ride?" she asks.

"The real question is, are *you* ready?"

Paris smiles mischievously, then takes off running up the steps to their bedroom. Neil follows, taking the steps two at a time until he catches up with her. He then swoops her up, and carries her to the bedroom kicking and screaming.

Belinda Walker-Graham

CHAPTER SIX

"Darn it. That girl is always prompt," Les says out loud as she gather her purse and keys.

Just as Les reaches the door, she stops. Maybe I should leave Steve a note, she thinks. At least it would be more than he left me. He got up early this morning and left without a word.

Before she can decide on what to do she hears the sound of Paris's horn a second time. "If that girl blows her horn again, I'm going to scream!" she says. At that moment she decides not to leave the note, and walks out the door. Leaving her worries behind, Les walks towards the car with a smile.

"So, what took you so long?" Paris asks.

"I was going to leave Steve a note until you became impatient," she answers.

"Well, let's roll," Paris says. "We don't want to be late. And where are we going anyway?"

"The building is located on Livernois, right before Outer Drive," she answers.

"Aren't you excited Les? I know I was when I first started my business."

"Extremely, girl. This is the beginning of what I've always dreamed of."

"Les, that's a dream many people have. Some of us are fortunate enough to achieve that dream. And I thank God everyday I was one of the fortunate ones. Starting a business is very frightening. Not knowing whether you're going to succeed or fail. And for me, it was very risky leaving a secure job for the unknown."

"Aren't you glad you took that risk?" Les asks.

"I am now," Paris answers. "But at first I wasn't so sure," she says softly. "Getting my travel agency off the ground was a lot of hard work. We both know what I was going through at the time."

Les nods in agreement. Paris continues. "But now I can look forward to the rewards, and a better future for Brian and Brandon."

"How are my bubbly nephews?"

"They're wonderful. I spoke with them last night."

"And how is Mrs. Findley?"

"Just fine," Paris answers. "A little lonely since Neil's dad passed away. But the boys kinda fill that void."

"Okay, we're almost there," Paris says. "Time to shake off the nerves and go in there with confidence."

Les takes a deep breath. "That man is putty in my hands."

"Thata girl," Paris responds, smiling. "So, do you have a name for your shop?"

"Sure do. I'm going to call it Leslie's Floral Shop."

"That's so original, Les," Paris laughs.

"Well, laugh at this," Les says, pointing. "You passed the only parking space available."

"That spot is two blocks away from the building."

"Paris, you are so lazy. I don't mind walking."

"Well I do," Paris responds, irritated. "Neil wore me out last night. I had my exercise for the week."

"I haven't. And I need all I can get."

"Are you talking exercise or sex?"

"Both," she answers, while rolling her eyes at Paris. "Now park the car and let's get going."

While walking towards the building, a well dressed man approaches them. "How are you ladies doing today?" he asks.

"Fine," they say, and continue walking past him.

"I know you're fine!" he yells.

Both Paris and Les look at each other and start laughing. "You can dress them up, but you can't take them out," Les comments.

"True dat," Paris responds.

"Are you talking Ebonic now? Or do you need to take up company with more adults, and less time with your boys?"

"Nah," Paris answers. "I wanted to show you how cool I am. As regards to my boys, they speak English, not Ebonic. I picked that up from Leonard."

"Like I said, you need to be around more adults," Les chuckles.

"Okay, you got me there. I learned quite a few things from Leonard."

"Please don't show Mr. Langley what you've learned," Les says, smiling as they walked through the door.

"Right on time," Mr. Langley says, extending his hand. "You must be Mrs. Wade?"

"Yes I am," Les responds. "And this is my sister Paris Findley."

"And how are you today?" he asks, taking Paris's hand.

"I'm doing fine," Paris answers. "This is such a nice building you have here, Mr. Langley."

"Why thank you, young lady. I put a lot of hard work into my business, and this building. Since we've grown so much, a larger building is necessary. Now

Mrs. Wade, we have business to discuss, and I have an appointment to make."

"By all means, lets get started," Les comments. With that, Mr. Langley directs them to his office.

Towards the end of their meeting, Mr. Langley says, "I like you, Mrs. Wade. I also like your ideas, and the plans you have for the place. It makes me feel good about renting my building to you."

"What?" Les says, stunned. "Are you telling me I'm your choice?" She grabs hold of Paris's hand.

"Yes, indeed I am," he answers. "That is, if you still want to rent the place. If so, it's all yours."

"Oh yes I do," she says, trying to contain herself.

"Well, it's settled," he says. "I'll have my attorney draw up the contract as soon as possible. I'd like to wrap this up quickly. Make sure you have your attorney go over the contract with you before signing."

"That's so kind of you to suggest that," Les says.

"Mrs. Wade, I am a fair man. I want you to know exactly what you're getting into."

"Thank you so much for giving me this opportunity."

"You're welcome," he responds. "I hope you have just as much success as I did in this building. Now, if you ladies will excuse me," he says, showing them the door. "I have an appointment to make. Oh, and young lady," he says, directing his attention to Paris. "I was very impressed with you during our tour. You asked the proper questions. I'm sure your business will succeed."

"Thank you Mr. Langley. With your vote of confidence, I'm sure it will. I know I'll do everything possible to make that a reality."

Mr. Langley smiles, then with a nod he walks away. As Paris and Les head towards the door, Les links her arm through Paris's and smiles. "I knew I made the right choice bringing you."

"Of course you did, Les," she responds. "You heard the man."

"I'm sure he was also impressed with that short skirt," Les comments. "As a matter of fact, he was more impressed with your legs than my ideas. He couldn't keep his eyes off of them, and was smiling throughout our meeting."

"That's how you got the building my sister," Paris says, then winks. "In all seriousness, Les, your ideas were wonderful. And I am proud of you. There was no way Mr. Langley could turn you down. And to be honest, he wasn't bad on the eyes either. A little on the short side, but oh so sexy. If I was single and into dating out of my race, I would have given that man my number."

"Well, for one, you're not single. And every man is a little on the short side for us, thanks to mom and dad."

As they continued to walk towards the car, the same man they had passed previously approaches them again. This time he stops.

"I just had to pause and tell you ladies how fine you both are. Like old wine. And by the way sister, that's a nice ride you have there."

"Thank you," Paris says, barely getting the words out.

After getting into the car, they both burst out laughing. "No, he didn't go there," Les laughs.

"Yes he did, and he compared you to old wine," Paris states.

"I think he was talking to the both of us," Les says.

"Nope, only you Les, because he knew you were the oldest."

"Look at him now, Paris," Les says, pointing. "He's trying to pick up that woman, and she's walking faster to get away. I bet he's singing that same 70s tune to her too."

"I'm sure he is," Paris answers. And I'm also sure that's the only suit he owns. I bet he puts it on everyday to walk up and down Livernois trying to pick up women."

"Look," Les says, laughing hysterically now. "The woman is kicking him, and hitting him with her purse."

As Paris drives off, they see the man running from the woman and waving for the bus to stop.

"I can't believe this," Paris says, laughing along with Les. "He has this nice suit on, trying to rap, and can't pick up a date."

"Yes he can," Les responds. "If the bus stops at your corner."

"Girl, shut up," Paris says, trying to drive and wiping the tears of laughter away. "So, where are we going for dinner tonight?"

"What about Greektown, Paris? The seafood pizza is so good!"

"That's a good idea Les. You're full of great ideas today. I haven't been to Greektown in a long time. You know, Greektown reminds me so much of the French Quarters in New Orleans."

"I've never been to New Orleans. I've always wanted to go there."

"Oh Les, you'd love it! The food is superb. Anyway, Greektown sounds like the place to go."

"Paris, maybe we should swing back by my place to call Ronnie and Alex to let them know. Speaking of Ronnie, she called this morning and said she had something to tell us."

"I hope she found a job," Paris responds. "That girl has too much time on her hands. Every time I'm in the middle of booking a trip for one of my customers, the phone rings. And you know who it is. Ronnie, asking what I'm doing. I want to say, 'Something you should be doing, working.'"

"Paris, give her a break. She's worked hard for many years, and she's probably not sure what she wants at this point in her life. And age plays an important role as well. She's competing with a lot of young women, fresh out of college."

Paris only nods her head in agreement. She's only half listening, thinking about the woman who's calling her home.

"Paris, you missed my street."

"I'll turn around."

"And here I thought you were listening to me."

"I was kinda listening, Les. I'm sorry. I didn't hear it all. You want to start over?"

"You must be losing your mind, Paris. The only time you'll hear it again is in your dreams. Now don't miss the turn again, because I don't want a tour of my neighborhood," she smiles.

As Paris pulls into the drive, Les notices Steve hasn't made it home. "I think I'll park on the street instead," Paris comments. "That way, I don't have to move my car when Steve arrives."

97

"It really doesn't matter," Les responds. "I'm sure he went out on one of the electrical jobs he had lined up. By the time he gets home, we'll be out of here. Let's get out of this car and make our calls."

After entering the house, Les notices she has messages. She walks over to the machine to retrieve them, while Paris goes into the kitchen to make coffee.

"Les, this is Alex," the first message says. "I left Michael and checked into a hotel. The number is 313-555-5655, room 1118. I'll explain at dinner."

Next, "Hi Leslie, this is Michael. I'm looking for Alex. If or when you see her, please ask her to call home, thank you."

"Paris!" Les yelled. "Get in here!"

Paris runs towards Les. "What's wrong?" she asks with concern.

"Alex has left Michael, girl!"

"What!" Paris is astonished. "Are you for real?"

"Yes, I'm for real. She left a message with her hotel and room number. And Michael called looking for her."

"Call the hotel to find out what's going on," Paris says, anxious to know the details.

"I'm only going to call to let her know where we're having dinner," Les says. "She made it very clear in her message that she'll explain tonight at dinner. But first, I'd like to cool out for a few minutes before I make the calls. There's been too much drama today. Is the coffee ready?"

"Sure is," Paris answers. "Let's go into the sun room, have coffee, and speculate."

"Hey Dad. Is this a good time to talk?"

"Yes son," he answers. "Your mother is out right now. So how did the trip go?"

"We're making progress, but we have problems, Dad."

"What kind of problems son?" he asks nervously.

"Calm down, Dad. Alex been snooping around."

"How could you let that happen, Michael? Don't you have control over your wife?"

"Oh, like you have control over mother."

"Don't sass me boy," he says harshly. "Now what happened?"

"I found pictures in a envelope, left on the bar. Our marriage is pretty shaky right now. I'm sure Alex hired a private investigator."

"You've made her suspicious of you, son. I'm sure she thinks you're having an affair. Look son," he says in a softer tone. "I like Alex, but I will not allow her to get in the way."

"Dad, I will handle Alex."

"You better had, son. We're getting too close to blow it now. We don't know how far Alex has gone with this. Or how much she knows."

"I'll find out, Dad. But in the meantime, we need to find other means of communication. We're taking a very big chance talking over the phone, which may be tapped."

"You're right, son. I'll be in touch soon."

"Okay Dad. I'll give you a call as soon as I get more information."

Michael hangs up the phone and walks over to the window. Oh God, he thinks, what am I to do? For starters, I need to find Alex. I can't explain everything to her right now, but at least I can try to squash some of her suspicions. I shouldn't have taken that later flight. If I had stayed on schedule, maybe we could have talked, and things wouldn't have gotten so out of hand. And why bring Preston into this? It's a good thing he was found out, and told to back off before he got too involved. I have to admit, he was clever enough to keep a roll of film. Alex, where are you?

As he heads back towards the phone, there's a knock on the door. "Yes Doris!" he yells.

"Mr. Crawford, there are two gentlemen here to see you."

"Thank you, Doris, please send them in."

It can't be, he says nervously to himself. I can't believe they came here, of all places.

The two men walk in with expressionless faces. "Hello gentlemen," Michael says, greeting them with a smile. "Please have a seat," he says pointing toward the wing chairs. "Thank you, Doris. And please close the door when you leave."

"Yes sir," she answers.

After the door closes, Michael lashes out. "What are you doing here?" he whispers harshly. "My wife could walk through that door any minute."

"I don't think so," says the heavyset balding fellow. "She checked into a hotel last night, or should I say very early this morning."

"We're here to give you info on your wife's whereabouts," says the taller man.

Michael looks dumbfounded as he stares at the taller man, with that ugly scar near his ear. The man stood up and took off his wire framed glasses. "Handle your business," he says, pulling out a hanky to clean his glasses. "Find out what she knows."

"And make sure you call us, rich boy, as soon as you find out," says the heavyset man, breathing hard as he lifts himself up from the chair.

Look at him, Michael says to himself. He's trying to threaten me, and he can hardly breathe.

As the two men head towards the door, the taller one hands Michael a piece of paper. "Use it," he says, and they walk out the door.

Michael looks down at the information. "So Alex," he says out loud. "This is where you're hiding out. Well, maybe I'll give you a visit. Doris!" he calls out.

"Yes sir," she answers, coming into the room.

"I'm stepping out for a while. If Mrs. Crawford calls, please inform her I shall return in a couple of hours."

That way, he thinks to himself, Alex won't think I'm tracking her down. And her guard will be down when I finally come face to face with her.

On his way to the hotel, all he can think about is getting his wife back home and ending this mess he's all caught up in. Since he knows the room number, he bypasses the desk and goes straight to the elevator.

When Michael finds himself facing the door, he composes himself, then knocks.

"Who is it?" a sweet voice asks.

"It's Michael."

"Go away Michael, I have nothing to say to you."

"Please Alex," he begs. "Don't leave me in the hallway begging."

"You need to beg, like the dog you are."

"Give me a chance to explain, please."

The door slowly opens, and Michael walks in. "Hello sweetheart," he says, walking towards Alex.

101

She steps back. "You have 15 minutes, Michael. So I suggest you start talking."

"I miss you very much," he starts.

"Liar," she says. "That's why you rushed home to be with me, your wife, right?"

Michael walks over to the bar to fix a drink. "Alex, I'm not having an affair."

"So you saw the pictures?"

"Yes I did, Alex. I'm sure you left them in view for the sole purpose of my finding them. Why didn't you come to me, Alex?"

"Oh, like you would confess if I had."

"There's nothing to confess," he responds. "I went to Chicago on business. The pictures you saw was not a romantic interlude, but a business deal."

"Don't insult my intelligence Michael. You met her in a park, not the office. Do you love her?"

"No sweetheart, I love only you," he answers softly.

"Then who was that woman you were with?"

"I can't explain it right now," he answers. "But what I'm working on will be over soon. Then I'll explain everything to you."

"Why did you come here, Michael?" she ask softly, choking back tears. "You claim you're not having an affair. What sense does that make?"

"I told you I'll explain when the time is right," he answers, now angry.

"Well, when the time is right for you, Mr. Crawford, it may not be for me," she shoots back. "I believe your time is up," she says, walking towards the door.

"Before I go, will you answer a question for me?" he asks.

Alex looks at him with her head cocked to the side, giving him a look that says, 'Go ahead, but make it quick.'

Michael clears his throat. "Why involve Preston in our business, Alex? Can you answer that for me please?"

"Why not? He's part of my family, and family takes care of each other. But that's something you wouldn't know about, Michael. Your family is so busy power struggling with each other, you've lost sight of what it means to protect and love."

"That's not a fair assessment," he comments.

"Michael," she screams, "I am not a client you're talking to! I'm your wife. This is exactly what I'm talking about. You don't know how to show emotions. We are not in a courtroom," she says, opening the door. "Please leave."

"I'm leaving, but I want you to know something," he responds. "I may not have a conventional family, but we do have feelings. It's just harder for us to express them."

They stare at each other for a second. When Alex turns her head to avoid looking at Michael, he walks out the door, closing it behind him. Alex stands frozen with tears streaming down her face.

Michael goes down the hall and enters the elevator. Just as the elevator door is about to close, it reopens. An attractive women enters.

"Strange bumping into you here, Michael," she says, smiling.

"What the hell are you doing here?" he asks with a surprised look.

"Now Michael, is that anyway to greet your friends?"

"Friends," he says, as if he's been insulted. "You're nothing to me. And answer my question," he demands, very angry now. "What are you doing here?"

"My, my. You sound rather testy," she says, avoiding his question. "Seems like I always bring out the best in you, and I wonder why, Michael," she says getting up close to his face. "But to answer your question," she says stepping back and winking, "I live here now."

"Why here?" he asks. "And why didn't you inform me of this in Chicago?"

"You're full of questions, aren't you?"

Before he can answer, the elevator door opens. They both step out of the elevator, and Michael grabs her arm and pulls her to the side.

"Take your hands off me," she says, snatching her arm away. "You don't want me to make a scene, now do you?"

Michael steps back without saying a word.

"Now that's more like it," she says, smoothing out her suit. "Look, I don't answer to you Michael. I am not your wife or employee. I call the shots, and I make the rules, so don't you forget it," she says with the force of having the upper hand.

"You enjoy making people lives miserable, don't you?" he asks. Leaning over to whisper in her ear, he continues. "Well, don't forget this. Your good thing will come to an end. That's a promise. And I always keep my promises."

Before she can open her mouth, he walks away.

"Well, well, Michael," she says, smiling to herself. "You do have balls after all. But not enough to control me. This will end only when I say it will end. And that won't be for a while yet, baby, I'm having too much fun."

Throwing her head back in laughter, she starts walking towards the restaurant.

After arriving home, Michael heads straight towards the study and slams the door. Pacing the floor while running his hand through his hair, he decides to place a call to his dad. When he picks up the phone, there's a voice already on the other end.

"How did it go?" the voice ask.

"Are you following my every move?" Michael asks, ignoring the question.

"Answer the question, rich boy."

"My wife only thinks I'm having an affair," Michael finally answers reluctantly. "But what's more important now, is that our friend is living in Michigan now. Why aren't you keeping track of her?"

"We already know, rich boy."

"What do you mean you already know?" Michael asks angrily. "Why didn't you tell me? What if my wife bumps into her at that hotel? Didn't you two brilliant men think of that?"

"Look, rich boy. Don't tell us how to handle our business. Anyway, how did we know your wife was going to up and leave? Since you're good at persuading a jury, we have every confidence you can persuade your wife to come back home. If you can't, we'll have to step in. I'm sure you don't want that to happen. We're banking on you, rich boy, to work your magic. We hope you're as good of an husband as you are an attorney. We'll be in touch." With that the man hangs up.

Michael places the phone down gently, trying to maintain his compose and not alarm Doris. "Damn," he says, trying to think of what to do next. He takes a deep breath and picks the phone back up to call his dad.

"Hello mother," he says dryly when she answers. "I need to talk to Dad."

"'Hello mother,'" she repeats back. "That's it. Not, 'How are you mother?' or, 'It's good to hear your voice mother.' I haven't talked to my only child in weeks, and that's all you have to say to me?"

"I'm sorry mother," he says. "I need to talk to Dad about an urgent matter."

"Anything I can help you with?"

"Thanks, but no, mother."

"Well Michael, it must not be about business. Because I'm well versed on legal matters, like your father is. So it must be about that wife of yours. You know Michael, you should come to me about those matters. But I guess you're afraid to, because your wife has turned you against me. I knew she was all wrong for you. She's uneducated and has no class. Darling, can't you see she's out of your league?"

"Stop it, mother," he says in a stern voice. "I will not listen to another word, and I don't know why I let you go on. That's my wife you're talking about. The women I love. I'm not asking you to love her, but I am telling you to show her some respect. And if you feel that's something you can't do," he hesitates, "then I will have nothing to do with you."

"How dare you talk to me in that manner, and with that tone of voice, Michael," she says with authority. "I am your mother."

"I apologize, mother. I didn't call to argue or upset you. I have a lot on my mind right now."

"Well, your father is out," she says, more calmly. "Why don't you fly out to Washington next weekend for a visit? And your wife too, of course," she says, as an afterthought. "I haven't seen you in such a long time."

"Next weekend is out of the question, mother. I have a lot on my plate. Let me talk to Alex first, and clear some of my workload, then we'll see. Is that okay with you?"

"I guess it will have to be," she answers. "I'll inform your father you called, Michael."

"Thank you mother, talk to you soon."

"Good-bye Michael."

After hanging up, Michael thinks back to what Alex had said. Alex was right, he says to himself. As much as I hate to admit it, my family doesn't know the meaning of love. I can't remember the last time my mother told me she loved me, or embraced me. When I passed the bar exam, Dad shook my hand and slapped me on the back. He also told me how proud he was. Mother, on the other hand, was nonchalant about my accomplishment. The only words that flowed out of her mouth was, how happy I made her by not disgracing the family. In a lot of ways I'm like my mother. And Alex picked up on that right away.

Oh, how I wish I could shower her with the kind of love she's used to. Her family is so loving. They welcomed me with open arms. Now, I must convince my wife to come back to a man who makes her so unhappy. That's going to be a feat in itself, but it must be done to protect her. But most importantly, I love her and want her home. I need to prove that I'm capable of loving her.

With that thought, Michael closes his eyes and drifts off to a long-awaited sleep.

Give Me the Simple Life

Belinda Walker-Graham

CHAPTER SEVEN

"I'm starved," Paris comments. "How much longer before dinner?"

"You still have time to kill, if that's what you want to know," Les answers.

"Well actually, I need to run by Neil's mom to check on the boys. They should be out of school by now."

"Give them a big kiss from auntie Les."

"I will, and I'll meet you guys at the restaurant around six."

As Paris drives off, Steve pulls into the drive. Darn it, Les says to herself. I didn't want to be here when he returned. In an effort to smooth things over, she steps onto the patio to greet him. "Hi sweetheart," she says with a smile. "Did you have a rough day? You look tired."

"I'm beat, it's been a long day," he answers. "Are you cooking today?

"Actually, I wasn't planning to," she answers. "My sisters and I are going to Greektown for dinner. But I can whip up something for you."

"That won't be necessary," he snaps. "Maybe I'll make plans and go out to dinner myself."

"That's not fair, Steve," she responds. "How could I tell you about my plans, when you left this morning without a word? Are we drifting that far apart where we can't even communicate anymore? I don't know what's happening between us, but I'm willing to try to get our marriage back on track."

Seeing that Steve was noncommittal, Les tries to reach him in a different way. "You know Steve, I miss the closeness and laughter we've shared. I miss telling you exciting news, like I got the building for the Floral Shop." She doesn't say another word, waiting for a response.

Finally Steve speaks. "Are you going through with it?"

"Yes I am. And I want you to be a part of it. This may be my dream, but you're my husband. And I want to share my dream with you."

"Look sweetheart," he says softly, looking directly into her eyes. "We have issues that we need to work through. There will be no future unless we resolve them."

Les goes into shock at that statement. "What do you mean Steve?" she stutters. "What are you trying to say to me?"

"Please calm down Les. What I'm trying to say, which is not easy, is that we need some time apart."

"For what Steve? Oh no," she says, throwing her hand up. "Are you seeing someone else?"

"No," he quickly answers. "I have never been unfaithful to you."

"Well what is it? Can't we work on whatever it is here, together?"

"Tell me how? We're like two ships in the night passing by, and not communicating with each other. Anyway, why are we discussing our private business on the patio? Let's go inside and continue this."

"There's nothing more to say," Les comments as she goes inside.

"Yes there is," he says, following her. "We have to discuss this."

Les stops to turn and face him. "I have tried to discuss our problems with you. But you always walk away. Now you have the nerve to come to me with a decision you, not we, made."

"Les, you know as well as I do, we can't continue to live like this. Someone had to make the decision to do something about our situation."

"And that someone was you. So I guess your mind is made up. When are you moving, Steve?"

"I'm going to a hotel tonight," he answers. "And don't worry, I'll continue to pay the bills."

"I'm not worried, I know you will," she says with conviction.

"Please don't make this harder than what it already is," he comments. "We won't be living in the same household, but we're still married, and I will handle my obligations. What I'm about to say maybe hard for you to swallow, but I am happy for you. You're a business woman now."

"If you're happy for me, then why don't you come over to the building with me? Not today of course, but maybe tomorrow."

"I'm not ready yet to get involved," he answers. "Give me some time to adjust to our new situation. We both need time and space."

"Steve, what will we tell the children?"

"For one thing, they're not children anymore, Les. They're adults with families of their own, and fully aware of life's ups and downs. Besides, what will we tell them? We're not sure ourselves what's going to happen. Why get them upset? This may only be temporary."

"I'm beginning to wonder how temporary this really is. I'm beginning to wonder if this separation is the beginning of the end for us," she says, with sadness in her voice.

"That will certainly happen if we don't put forth the effort to work on our marriage," he responds. "I guess it is a good thing the kids live out of state. That way they can't watch us go through this low point in our marriage."

"So when are you going to gather your things?"

"I threw a few items in a duffel bag this morning."

"I see you didn't waste any time," she comments, with raised eyebrows.

Ignoring the remark, he continues. "I'll pack the rest of my things this evening."

"That's fine with me," she responds. "I'm leaving for dinner around 5:30. You can collect your things then. And since your mind is made up to move out, I prefer that you're gone when I return."

He nods his head in agreement and heads towards the door. When he reaches it, he stops. "It's for the best, you know," he says, then walks out.

Les stares in disbelief, not knowing what to make of what just happened. In a zombie-like state, she heads towards the bedroom to dress for dinner.

"What are you boys doing home?" Paris asks. "It's a good thing I came home first."

"Hi mom," they both say in unison.

"Didn't I tell you two to go over to your grandmother after school? You know I don't like you being home alone."

"We went to Grandma's after school," Brian answers. "Dad picked us up."

"And where is your dad?"

"He went to the store." Brandon answers this time.

"Yeah, sure did," Brian says. "Dad told us you were going to dinner with aunt Leslie, aunt Ronnie, and aunt Alex."

"So we're going to have boy's night out, since you're having girl's night out," Brandon pipes in.

"Come over here you two and give me a hug and a kiss," she commands.

"Okay," Brian says. "But we can't do this in public."

"Yeah," Brandon says, going along with his brother. "If anyone ever saw us being kissed by our mother, we'd get teased bad."

"Well, I don't want you two to get teased or embarrassed. I promise to only hug and kiss you in private. Deal?" she asks, holding out her hand for them to come shake it.

"It's a deal," they both say, and run over to give her a hug.

"Oh, mom," Brandon says, releasing his grip. "Some woman called."

"Really," she says, with widening eyes. "And what did she want?"

"I don't know. She asked to speak to dad. When I told her dad was busy, she said she'd call back. She also said she looked forward to meeting us."

"Are we having company from out of town?" Brian asks.

"No Brian, we are not," she answers.

"Did we do good, mom?" Brandon asks. "You always tell us not to let anyone know we're home alone."

"Yes you did, boys," she says with a smile. "I'll make sure to give your dad the message. Now, how was school today?" she asks, changing the subject.

"School was fun," Brian answers, excited.

"And before you ask," Brandon pipes in, "we don't have any homework today."

"Well, maybe I should give you two a few math problems to keep you on your toes," she says, trying to look serious.

"Oh no, mom," Brian says with a worried look. "We'd rather clean our rooms instead."

"Gotcha," she says, laughing. "So let's go and get those rooms cleaned."

"Big mouth," Brandon says to Brian.

Moving very slowly, the two boys head toward the stairs. Paris runs behind them to move them along. When the boys see her, they start laughing and run up the stairs to their rooms.

Paris turns around smiling, and walks back into the family room. When she hears the door shut, she stops smiling.

"Where is everyone?" Neil calls out. He walks into the family room, where he find Paris sitting by the fireplace. "Hi baby," he says walking over to give her a kiss.

"Hi yourself," she says back, receiving his kiss.

"So how was your day?" he asks, walking over to the sofa.

Paris doesn't hear his question, she's busy watching his butt as he walks to the sofa. That man looks so good in those tight jeans, she says to herself. Tall and handsome, with the perfect butt. Snap out of it, girl. Fantasizing about his butt, and how good he looks, doesn't erase the fact that he could be having an affair for the second time.

"Sweetheart, I asked, how was your day?"

"Oh, I'm sorry Neil. It was interesting. I went with Les to get a building for her floral shop."

"Did she get it?"

"Yes she did. The landlord was very impressed with her and the ideas she had. He made the decision right on the spot."

"Tell Les congratulation for me."

"I sure will. Before I forget, you had a call. Brandon took the message."

"Okay, I'll get the message from Brandon in a minute. Right now, I'm going to spend some quality time with my beautiful wife."

"Sweetheart, I wish we could spend more time together, but I need to get ready for dinner. I'm going to be late as it is."

"No sweat, we can continue our quality time together when you get home tonight."

"Neil, I'm sure it's going to be rather late when I get home. And we both have to get up early."

"I don't care how late you get in or how early we have to get up." He winks at her. "I'm waiting up for my wife tonight."

I hate to burst your bubble, she thinks to herself, but I'm going to lay something on you, and it won't be me.

"While you're getting ready," he continues, "I'll go to Brandon's room and get that message."

As he stood up to leave, she stops him. "Wait!" she shouts, not happy she's forced to tell him now. "There's no need. Brandon gave me the message. Brian thought we were having a visitor from out of town."

"Why, did aunt Ruth call? You know it's around the time she visits."

"I'm very doubtful it was aunt Ruth, since she didn't identify herself. This woman also expressed an desire to meet our boys." Paris stops talking to see his expression. Check him out, she says to herself, looking very puzzled with his head cocked to the side. He's a good actor.

"Paris, I have no idea who this woman is," he says.

"Well, I suggest you find out," she says harshly. "This is not the first time we've gotten strange calls. I've had hang ups, name calling, and a woman claiming she had the wrong number. And now this! I really don't want to accuse you of anything, especially after everything we've gone through. But if by any chance you're seeing another woman, you better warn her she's treading on dangerous grounds when it comes to my babies."

"I swear to you, Paris, I'm not having an affair. I made a promise to you that it would never happen again. I love you baby," he says, pleading for her to believe him.

"Tell me Neil, what's love got to do with it when you're thinking from that thing dangling between your legs, and not your heart?"

"Sweetheart, I'm not going to risk losing you and those boys for anyone." Taking a deep breath, Neil knew it was time to be honest. "Come over here and sit next to me please. I need to talk to you about something."

Paris obeys reluctantly and sits down, all the while thinking how she is going to react to his confession. "Oh honey," he says taking both of her hands into his. "I know you need to get dressed, and this may not be the appropriate time to discuss this, but you need to know what's going on. I thought I handled the problem. But since our boys are being dragged into this, it's time to clue you in on what's going on."

Looking into Paris's eyes, he could see he was frightening her. He thinks, She look so fragile right now. How I wish I didn't have to tell her this, but I must. He gathers up enough strength to continue.

"Paris, I will not jeopardize my family because of the mistakes I've made," he says holding his head down in shame. Lifting his head up and looking her square in the eyes, he continues. "Remember the night I went out for pizza?"

"Yes," she answers softly, her heart pounding.

"Well," he continues, "I received a call on my cell phone while waiting on the pizza. I thought it was you calling, wondering what was taking so long or if I was okay. But it was Marlene."

Paris tries to move her hands away, but he holds on tighter. "Please let me finish," he begs.

Paris rolls her eyes up towards the ceiling, trying to keep the tears from falling.

"Marlene wants to resume the relationship, Paris. I told her that was impossible. That I'm back where I belong. With my wife, my family. But she didn't want to hear that. It's like she's obsessed. Then she really laid one on me. She's here, living in Michigan."

Upon hearing this, Paris forcefully removes her hands out of his grip, jumps up, and heads towards the door. Neil jumps up to go after her.

"Paris, don't leave," he begs.

"What else is there to say, Neil? I'm running late, and I don't even have time to get dressed."

"Please don't do this, sweetheart, I've done nothing wrong. I didn't break my promise to you."

"Neil, now is not the time," she says softly. "I'm not saying I don't believe you, I just need time to absorb all of this. We'll talk when I get home."

"Okay," he says, finally giving up. "But we will finish this conversation tonight."

She turns her back to him. "Brian, Brandon," she calls out. "Come give mom a kiss, I have to go now."

The boys run down the stairs to hug and kiss their mom. "You two have a good time with your dad, and I'll see you in the morning, okay?"

"Okay mom," they both said cheerfully and at the same time. "You have fun too."

"I will," she answers, and walks out the door.

Looking back as she walks to the car, she can see Neil standing there with his arms around the boys. She then becomes angry at Marlene.

Messing with my boys, she says to herself. If I ever run into her, I'm going to beat her down. The nerve of that woman, calling my home harassing me. Even though I believe Neil, all of this would not be happening if he hadn't picked up that nutty woman. Now me and my babies are drawn into this mess he's made. All I can say is, he better take care of this problem or else I'll be forced to handle this myself. For right now, a drink is what I need.

Watching Paris drive away brings sadness to Neil's eyes. She's hurting, he says to himself. And it's all my fault. I can't allow this to happen a second time. I've got to do something about this. But how? Marlene is so delusional right now. I'll never get through to her. But I've got to try.

"Dad, I'm hungry," Brandon says, interrupting Neil's train of thought.

"Me too," Brian pipes in, following the lead of his brother.

"Alright boys," Neil responds. "Let's go back inside and order a pizza."

"Yeah!" they both scream.

"Why don't you boys go pick out a movie to watch while I order the pizza?"

"Okay," Brian answers and run to pick out a movie, with Brandon on his heels.

After ordering the pizza, Neil thinks back to the time he met Marlene.

I should have known she was trouble when I bumped into her at the airport, he says to himself. Little did she know, I was on to her. Dropping those bags was done on purpose. But I played along, because I was searching for some excitement in my life. Paris and I had reached a dead end. We had nothing left to offer each other. Marlene brought me back to life. She was exciting and willing to do anything for me, and to me. I was becoming addicted to her. She had endless energy. We would party the night away, then make love until dawn. Marlene was wild, and she brought out the animal in me. I began to do things I never thought I would do, like having sex in the men's room.

I had no idea she was in there. While washing my hands after taking a leak, I felt someone rubbing up against me. My natural instincts to attack kicked in. I turned to look into the face of Marlene, smiling seductively. At that point I was beginning to get really turned on. Marlene started slowing unzipping my pants, and that was all it took. We fumbled our way into the stall, and it was on.

But there was another side to Marlene. The one that was more dangerous than just taking a risk. Hanging out with shady people and places was not my thing. But it definitely was Marlene. She would sweet talk me into going to the worst kind of bars, which made me rather nervous. I have no problem in defending myself, or her for that matter. But I don't like to be put into situations where it might become necessary. She always rejected my suggestion of going to a nice restaurant or a popular night club. I thought women loved going to exclusive places, but Marlene proved me wrong. I never could figure that one out until the night we went out for a carryout.

As usual, she decided against going to a sit down restaurant and opted to get a take out from this soul food place called the Rib Shack. I wanted to push the issue of going to a nice place for once, but I could see her mind was made up. Plus, she was in a bad mood from a call she had received earlier. I tried to get her to talk about it, but she blew me off, so I left it alone. However, I did overhear some of the conversation, in reference to a package. I started to bring it up during the ride to the south side of town to pick up our food, but Marlene was so quiet, I decided against it.

After arriving to our destination and parking, I noticed a hooker and a man I assumed was her pimp, on the side of the small building. They both stopped talking and turned to stare at Marlene and myself. Leery of getting out of the car, I slowly opened the door, only to be stopped by Marlene. She insisted on going in to get our food, which I thought was rather strange. Marlene always insisted I go and pay for the food.

As a safety measure, I watched Marlene walk into the restaurant, then I started looking around. You never know who might sneak up on you in this neighborhood.

I turned back around just in time to see Marlene and the pimp exchange a package for money. Here I am looking around in case someone tries to jack me, and my so-called woman is jacking me in a different way. I'm not a street man, but I do know when something is going down.

As Marlene started to walk away, the man grabbed her arm. Seeing her in danger, I snatched open the car door to jump out and protect her, until I saw a metal object come out of her purse. I stopped in my tracks and stared in disbelief. At that moment, I realized Marlene was fully capable of protecting herself. I also realized the mistake I'd made abandoning my family. This was not the life I wanted. And if I continued on this path, I might not have the opportunity to correct the wrong I'd done.

From that moment on, I decided to distance myself from Marlene. When she returned to the car I pretended as if I was nodding. I even went as far as jumping to attack when she opened the car door. I never asked Marlene about that night. It was unimportant to me, since I was going to end the relationship.

But to my surprise, ending it wasn't going to be easy. I was more addicted than I thought. Every time I found the courage to end it all, somehow I'd end up in her bed. Some would say I was a glutton for punishment. That's why it was such a blessing when Paris busted us. Little did she know, she was doing me a favor. I was able to do what I should have done a long time ago, leave and go back to where I belonged, with my family.

I wanted to tell Paris that after we got back together, but I was afraid she would look at me and see a coward and not a man. That's how I saw myself. At one point in my life I had been on top of the world. Having a family and a career was what I'd always striven for. And by the grace of God, I was blessed with both. And double blessed with not one, but two handsome boys. My parents were so proud of me. I was proud of myself. But my father was especially proud. As long as I can remember, my father instilled in me the meaning of being a man. And boy, was he a good example. He was a great man, a devoted husband and father.

It seems like everything he taught me went out the door long before the affair. When and how that happened is beyond me. It's sad to say, but I'm glad Dad's not around to see the mess I'd made of things. Instead of becoming the man he worked so hard to make me, I'd become a coward. I couldn't face the problems Paris and I had, so I escaped into the arms of Marlene. It was so easy to walk away from the woman I loved, but not from the woman I lusted for. That just shows how messed up I was. But not anymore. Now is the time to step up to the plate and be a man.

With that thought Neil stares into space, not hearing the boys sneak upon him. "Grrrrrr…" they growl, trying to scare him.

Pretending to be really frightened, he jumps. "You guys almost made me run out of my skin!" he says.

They both start laughing hysterically. "We really scared you, didn't we Dad!" Brian says.

"You sure did," he answers. "And you probably scared the pizza man away too!"

"See what you did," Brandon says, worried. "Now we might not get to eat. I told you we shouldn't scare Dad."

"Don't worry Brandon," Neil says, chuckling to himself. "I see a car pulling up right now. I think we're going to have pizza after all."

"Yaah!" they both yell in unison.

Neil stands up, pats both boys on their heads playfully, and goes to meet the pizza man.

"Okay," he says after shutting the door. "Let's watch that movie you two picked, and grub on some pizza."

"Yeah," Brian says, excited. "This is our night!"

Belinda Walker-Graham

CHAPTER EIGHT

Where is everyone? Ronnie asks herself. I'm always waiting on Alex and Les, but Paris is always on time. It's been 45 minutes. I can't wait to tell everyone the news. And wait until they see this 3-carat diamond ring I'm sporting. Holding her hand out in front of her, she stares at the diamond ring with a smile on her face.

"Excuse me," the waiter says politely. "Would you like a drink while you're waiting for the rest of your party?"

"No, not yet, but thank you anyway," she answers.

Then, as the waiter is about to walk away, Ronnie sees Alex. "Sir," she says loudly to get the waiter's attention, "can you please direct the woman in the red dress over to this table?"

"Yes ma'am," he answer and walks over to Alex, then points towards Ronnie. As Alex walks towards the table, Ronnie notices how good she looks. Then Ronnie says to herself, Too bad that beautiful dress can't cover the sadness on her face.

As Alex approaches, Ronnie perks up. "Well, finally. I thought I was going to have dinner all by my lonesome."

"Sorry I'm late," Alex responds. "I took a nap and forgot to set the alarm."

"Are you feeling okay?" Ronnie asks. "It's not like you to take a nap. You're always busy doing something."

"Ronnie, I left Michael," she pipes in.

"What happened when you confronted him?" Ronnie asks, trying to stay composed for Alex's sake.

127

"To be honest, I didn't. After I saw the pictures, I left before he returned home."

"Alex! You didn't give him a chance to explain."

"Well, yes and no."

"What do you mean, yes and no?"

"He found out somehow where I was staying and showed up. After a little time to myself to absorb all of this, I would have eventually confronted him. Anyway, he told me he wasn't having an affair, but didn't want to tell me who the woman was, or why they met in a park and not the office."

"So you've drawn your own conclusion?"

"What would you call it!" Alex shouts. Looking around she continues with a whisper, "She's definitely not a client."

"Wow, this is unbelievable," Ronnie says, shocked. "He didn't give you any explanation?"

"No," Alex answers. "That's the sad part of this mess. He was saying over and over how he was going to tell me everything when the time was right. So I informed him that when the time was right, it might be too late for us. I love him Ronnie, but I'm not going to let him make a fool out of me."

"I hear you girl," Ronnie responds. "I see Les and Paris coming in the door."

As Ronnie stands to flag them, she see the waiter pointing in their direction.

"Hey, my sisters," Paris says as they reach the table.

"It's about time," Ronnie remarks. "If I was a drunk, I'd be smashed by now waiting on you."

"You are a drunk," Paris chuckles.

"I don't think so, Alex is," Ronnie replies.

"Is that so?" Alex says. "By the end of the night we'll see who the drunk really is."

"I got news for you, my sisters," Les states. "All of you are drunks. I'm the only one in the family who knows her limit."

"You're also the only one in the family still doing the cabbage patch on the dance floor," says Ronnie.

Everyone starts laughing. "You're too funny Ronnie," Les comments. "Maybe you can get a job as a comedian, since you're in need of a job."

"That was a low blow, Les," Ronnie responds. "I see you're trying to get some spunk. For your information, I may have a job."

"That's wonderful!" Alex says, excited.

"Where, and doing what?" Paris asks.

"I'd be in complete charge of running a clothing store called Maze," she answers.

"You've got to be kidding!" Les replied excitedly. "That place is the talk of Detroit. I heard they also have a spa, and serve you lunch and champagne."

"That's the store, Les," Ronnie responds. "The owner is opening up another store in New York and needs someone to oversee the store here in Detroit."

"How did you get such a good lead on that job?" Alex asks.

"My future husband," she answers, holding out her hand. Everyone gasps.

"What a beautiful ring," Paris says, taking hold of Ronnie's hand to get a closer look.

"Congratulations girl!" Alex screams, grabbing her sister around the neck.

"You deserve to be happy," Les says, with tears in her eyes. "You've sacrificed a lot to be with Preston.

I'm glad he finally did the right thing by asking you to marry him. I'm happy for the both of you."

"I'm sorry to interrupt such a Kodak moment, but did our waiter forget about us? Paris asks.

"I was wondering the same thing," Alex comments.

Paris signals for the waiter. "Didn't I say you were all drunks?" Les giggles. "Can't wait to get a drink, can you?"

"As you can see, we don't have to wait for long," Ronnie says, pointing towards the waiter."

"I'm sorry ladies," he says. "We're quite busy tonight. What can I get for you this evening?"

"Chardonnay," Alex answers.

"And for me also," Ronnie says.

Paris orders a Long Island ice tea. When Les orders scotch on the rocks, everyone looks at her.

"Why is everyone staring at me?" she asks.

"Because we're the drunks, remember?" Ronnie says.

The waiter cleared his throat to get their attention. "Can I get you ladies anything else?"

They all placed orders for appetizers. The waiter left, and soon returned with their drinks and appetizers.

"Goodness, Les," Alex comments, "the waiter just sat the drinks down and your glass is half empty already. Maybe you should ease up a little, after all you're not much of a drinker."

Les threw up her hand to wave off Alex's comment, and took another sip.

"Okay Alex, 'fess up," Paris says. "Inquiring minds want to know."

"Know what?"

"Why are you in a hotel?"

Before answering, Alex takes a sip of wine. After setting the glass down, she starts to explain.

"Michael's cheating on me. I became suspicious and hired Preston to investigate. He followed Michael to Chicago and brought back evidence."

"Wow, this is like in the movies," Les says, signaling the waiter for more drinks.

"This is really deep," Paris comments. "But you didn't need to hire Preston. I would have done it for free."

"Yes, we know about your work, Paris," Ronnie says. "You're such a professional."

"I got the information I needed, now, didn't I?" Paris responds smugly.

"Yeah, along with a keepsake," Alex says.

"I'm sure she didn't miss those few braids I pulled out," Paris responds. "Anyway, I brought them back with me to give to Ronnie. She can use some extra hair."

"Thanks but no thanks," Ronnie says, patting her hair. "Besides, if I wanted long hair I would never have cut it."

"I bet you miss folks mistaking you for Lela Rochon," Alex comments. "You got a kick out of that."

"I'm over that now," Ronnie replies. "Getting off of me, I think Paris needs to mail back Miss Thang's hair. I'm sure she can use it, considering the cost of fake hair these days."

Everyone starts laughing except for Les. "Les, are you alright?" Ronnie asks with a concerned look.

"She's doing just fine from the looks of it," Paris answers. "That's her third drink."

"None of you know what you're talking about," Les says, slurring her words. "I heard everything you guys said. About the hair and all. Thanks to momma, we all have enough to give a lot of folks, except for baldy over there. So are you all satisfied now? I was somewhat listening."

"But you were somewhere else too," Paris notes.

"My life is falling apart," Les blurts out. "Steve moved out."

They all look at her with wide eyes and open mouths.

"This is the second," she hesitates to gather her thoughts, "second time you've all stared at me. Do I look like an alien or something?" she asks, weaving noticeably in her chair.

"No," they say in unison, giggling.

"But you do look like the drunk you called us," Alex comments.

"Look at all of our lives right now," Les goes on, with her eyes half shut. "I'm sitting here drowning my sorrows, which I add, Alex should be doing the same. Ronnie is celebrating her upcoming nuptials. And Paris, well, Paris is trying to be the next heavyweight champion."

"Well Les, all I have to say is that I had my pity party at the hotel," Alex responds. "But you're still up on me with the drinks. I've only had two, but Ronnie is running neck and neck with you. She's on her third glass of wine."

"I have an excuse," Ronnie responds, holding up her glass. "I'm celebrating."

"In that case, let's all make a toast to Ronnie," Les says loudly, trying to stand.

"Easy does it!" Paris blurts out, trying to catch Les before she hits the floor. "Your drinks are cut off, and hand over your keys."

"No!" Les shouts.

Ronnie walks over to her side of the table to get the keys herself. While they're struggling with Les's purse, Paris turns around to see who's staring at them, and notices a woman in a leopard suit walk into the restaurant. "She looks familiar," Paris says.

"Who looks familiar?" Alex asks.

"That woman who just walked into the restaurant," Paris answers. "I know her from somewhere."

"There's so many people standing around, I can't see who you're talking about," Alex comments.

Staring very hard at the woman, Paris suddenly remembers. "I know who she is now! Different hair style but same face!" she exclaims, now steaming.

"What are you talking about?" Ronnie asks as she finally snatches the purse out of Les's hands.

When Paris opens her mouth to answer, the words that come out are, "Catch her!"

It's too late. Les is on the floor after falling out of the chair when Ronnie snatched her purse. Jumping up, Alex goes to pick Les up off the floor. "Ronnie, help me!" she screams. "People are watching us."

"That's her," Paris says, pointing. "That's Miss Thang, who Neil had the affair with."

"How do you know?" Alex asks, breathing hard while helping Les back into the chair. "It's dimly lit in here."

"That's Marlene," Paris answers. "And I'm going to tell her a thing or two."

133

"For what?" Ronnie shouts. "It's been a year since the affair."

"Maybe for Neil, but not for her. She's been harassing me and involving my babies in this mess. Oh, it's on!" With that she charges over towards Marlene, passing the manager on his way to their table.

"I think we're in trouble," Ronnie comments. "The manager is headed this way, Alex."

"Oh no," she says frantically. "We're going to get thrown out of here. This is so embarrassing."

"Calm down, Alex. Maybe he won't throw us out. Les is quiet now."

"She should be!" Alex exclaims. "She's knocked out, look at her. She's sleeping on our table, and snoring. And with Paris getting ready to act ghetto, we're out of here for sure. All I wanted was a quiet dinner with my sisters," Alex says with tears in her eyes. "This is a circus, and our parents didn't teach us to act like clowns."

"Us!" Ronnie shouts. "What about you, Miss Prim and Proper. Anyway, I don't have time for this. I need to get to Paris before she makes a scene. You handle the manager. I hope I can reach Paris before she makes a fool of herself. With that she rushes after Paris.

The closer Ronnie gets, the louder the voices become. "Oh my God!" she says. "Is that Paris I hear?"

"You're a slut!" Paris screams. "You're calling my home harassing me. Telling my boys you're going to meet them. You're a nut case, and don't know how to let go! You need help, my sister."

"Who in the hell you think you're talking to!" Marlene screams back. "Coming to me with all these lies!"

"It's not a lie and you know it," Paris shoots back. "Neil doesn't want you! Get that through your crazy bald head."

"I think you better get out of my face," Marlene responds, more calmly. "Your soon to be ex-husband don't want you. He loves me, and he told me that the night he stopped by. You know the night I'm talking about. He's going to leave you again for me. And this time we will be a family, along with your precious babies."

Paris stands there seething as Marlene continues. "And guess what else," she says, smiling. "He told me all of this after we made love."

"Liar!" Paris screams.

As Ronnie gets closer, her heart starts beating faster. I know that tone, she says to herself. Paris is ready to strike. Ronnie starts moving faster.

But it's already started. When Ronnie reaches the scene there's a crowd of people, and someone is yelling, "Cat fight!"

"Oh no, I'm too late," Ronnie blurts out as she pushes her way through the crowd. Finally reaching her destination, she stands frozen for a second as she sees Paris and this Marlene person rolling on the floor. Paris has on this very short skirt, which at this point has risen to her waist due to the scuffling. Marlene has only one shoe on, and her wig is twisted, but is still on her head. Two guys are trying to pull them apart.

Snapping out of her initial shock, Ronnie starts reacting by hitting the guy grabbing her sister. "Leave my sister alone!" she yells as she tries to push him off Paris. The guy reacts by pushing back, knocking Ronnie into the crowd. Then he manages to pull Paris, kicking and screaming, off Marlene.

Ronnie regroups and rushes to her sister. "Are you okay?" she asks, hugging her.

"I'm fine," Paris answers, breathing hard while straightening her clothes.

"I'll be right back," Ronnie says as she head towards Marlene. She spots Marlene adjusting her wig.

When Marlene looks up, she's staring Ronnie in the face. "I suggest you leave my sister and her family alone." Ronnie hisses. "And when I say family, I mean my nephews too."

"Get out of my face, bitch," Marlene snaps. "You don't know who you're dealing with."

Getting right in Marlene's face, Ronnie snarls, "And you don't know who you're dealing with. You see, I'm not like my sister Paris. There'll be no rolling on the floor. I'll make sure you never bother my sister again. And trust me when I say, I do have connections. I don't know what you're up to, but if I were you, I'd rethink it. Because the outcome wouldn't be worth it."

With that, Ronnie walks away. When she reaches Paris, she grabs her arm and pulls her to the side.

"What is your problem?" Ronnie demands. "And why did you let that woman get to you like that?"

"We exchanged words, and one thing led to another. I'm so embarrassed, Ronnie," she says shamefully.

"Well, you should be," Ronnie replied softening her tone. "That was quite immature, and no man is worth you fighting over, and showing all of your jewels to the world."

"At least what they saw was pretty and clean," Paris responds, managing a smile. "You know momma always told us to wear nice and clean underwear, because you never know what may happen."

"Come on, silly girl," Ronnie says, her anger subsiding. "Let's collect our things, get Alex and Les, then get out of here."

As they head towards the table, they spot Alex struggling to help Les walk, and the manager walking alongside them, with their belongings.

"Paris, I do believe we're being booted out," Ronnie comments.

"I'm sorry guys," Alex says as she gets closer, still breathing hard. "We have to leave. I couldn't reason with the manager."

Clearing his throat to get all their attention, the manager hands over their things. "I suggest you ladies not visit this establishment for at least six months. You have caused too much disruption. Now I'm sure you can find your way out," he says, gesturing with his hand in the direction of the door.

"My God Paris, what happened to you?" Alex asks.

"Yeah," Les says, looking up with a silly grin on her face. "You don't have that pretty long braid anymore."

Ignoring Les, Alex continues. "Your hair is all over your head. You made a fool out of yourself, didn't you?"

"Alex, I'd rather not discuss it right now, if you don't mind," Paris says, throwing up her hand to dismiss the question. "Let's just get out of here."

As they exit the restaurant, Alex points towards a limousine. In unison, they turn to look at Alex, then Les.

"Don't look at me like that!" Alex exclaims. "I wanted to come in style. And I figured since drinking would be involved, the limo might be needed. Case in point," she says, looking in Les's direction. "You guys know I don't believe in drinking and driving."

Still staring at her, not believing a word, Ronnie speaks up. "Why are you trying so hard to convince us? We know you, Alex. And there's more to it than you wanting to be conscious of the law all of a sudden."

"Okay," Alex says, fidgeting like a kid caught telling a lie. "I was serious about the drinking and driving, but there's more to it. I wanted to stick it to Michael with the bill, by using the same limo service he uses, and charging it to his account."

"That sounds more like it," Ronnie says.

"You go girl," Les slurs, throwing her arm in the air, which causes her to lose her balance.

"Grab her!" Paris screams. "We better get this drunk home and in bed before she pass out again."

"I agree," Alex replies. "Everybody get in, we're calling it a night."

After watching the limo pull off, Marlene turns around and comes face to face with the manager.

"Miss, are you all right?" he asks.

"Yes," she says, very nastily.

"We apologize about what happened tonight, and your tab is on us. Is there anything else we can do for you, miss?"

"What you can do is make sure those bitches never come back," she answers.

"We've taken care of that," he responds. "Now, if I can direct you to your table," he says, taking the lead and heading towards her table. After seating her the manager instructs her to call upon him when she's ready to order, then walks away.

"Oh Miss Paris," Marlene says to herself while patting her hair. "You haven't seen the last of me. I may have other business to handle, but you're definitely on my list. So for now, go on home. I can see you running into Neil's arms crying."

The door slams and Paris walks into the family room. "What in God's name happened to you?" Neil asked. "Were you mugged?" He walks over to her with concern.

"Don't touch me or come near me!" she screams. "It's because of you I'm looking a mess," she says, crying.

"Honey, calm down and tell me what happened," he says, stepping back.

"Your lover is what happened."

"Marlene!" he says, shocked.

"Yes Marlene," she answers. "I ran into her at Greektown. We scuffled, as you can see."

"That's it!" he yells, walking over to grab his jacket. "I'm going down to the police station to get a restraining order on that crazy woman."

Standing there watching Neil, Paris realizes how serious he is. "Get back here, Neil," she says softly. "Not tonight. Let's just go to bed, I'm really tired. It can wait until tomorrow, we'll go together."

He walks up to her, takes her into his arms, and gently kisses her forehead. "Let's get you cleaned up, and go to bed." She nods and they both go upstairs.

"Hey baby, I didn't hear you come in. How was dinner?"

"Preston, let me tell you, it was a night to remember," Ronnie answers while kicking off her shoes.

"Were you all able to cheer up Alex?"

"It turns out that Alex didn't need a lot of cheering up, Les did," she answers. "Problems with Steve, she told us."

"Not Les," he says, surprised. "They have one of the best marriages I know of."

"Or so we thought," she comments. "There's trouble in paradise, big trouble. Baby Steve moved out. He actually left my sister."

"When, Ronnie?"

"Today is what Les told us, and she is bombed out. She was drinking scotch on the rocks. I can't even remember how many she had."

"You probably can't remember because you weren't far behind," he says, smiling.

"Oh shut up," she says, and playfully hits him with a pillow. "Anyway, she was so drunk, Preston, that she fell out of the chair," she says laughing.

"Was she hurt?"

"Baby, I don't think she felt a thing," she answers, laughing even harder.

"Come on Ronnie, that's not funny. She could have been seriously hurt."

"Well, if she was, we wouldn't have known because after getting her back into the chair, her head hit the table and she was out."

Now Preston joins in on the laughter. "With all that commotion, I'm surprised you all weren't thrown out," he comments. "That's too classy of a place to carry on like that."

"Oh, but we were thrown out," she responds. "But not until after the brawl."

"There's more to this story?"

"Oh yes, there is. Paris spotted the woman Neil had the affair with. She says this woman has been harassing her. And even talking to the boys over the phone. So she confronted the woman. Next thing I know, they were rolling on the floor."

"Wow, what a night! Just think, if you'd stayed home with me, you would have missed all the fun."

"What fun? That was work! I broke a sweat dealing with those two. It's a good thing Alex gave us all a ride home in the limo, because I exerted so much energy I wouldn't have been able to drive home."

"And let's not forget the drinking and driving," he reminds her.

"Okay, you made your point," she responds. Ronnie then cuddles up to Preston. "Baby, I'm worried about my sisters. And I've never seen Les like that before. She's really hurting, and I don't know what I can do to help ease her pain."

"You can't baby, only time can do that."

"What about Paris and Alex?" she asks. "Paris is tough and impulsive. Nothing she did tonight really surprised me. Alex used to be that way somewhat."

"What way?"

141

"You know, spunky. She's never been impulsive, but she had guts. She's so meek now. Letting Michael treat her the way he has is totally out of character for her."

"Look Ronnie, I'm not trying to defend the guy, but maybe there's a reasonable explanation for his behavior. We don't know what's going on. Don't be so quick to pass judgment."

"It's not that I dislike Michael, or any of my brother-in-laws. But when I see my sisters in pain, and their husbands are partially to blame, then my primary concern is for my sisters."

"That's understandable," he responds. "So I guess our great news came at the wrong time?"

"I'm afraid so, and I'm ashamed to admit this, but I was angry over the fact they were so engrossed in their own problems."

Preston kisses her gently on her lips and holds her close to him. Pulling away a little to look into his face, she continues. "I know they're happy for me. But I guess their problems are so overwhelming they can't hide the sadness, even for me. Oh baby, promise we'll always keep the lines of communication alive."

"You got it baby," he answers. "I don't want to make the same mistakes I made in my first marriage." Looking up to the ceiling he continues. "Although I didn't have much to go on."

"You told me your grandmother was wonderful," she responds.

"Don't get me wrong baby," he replies. "Grandma was my rock, and very loving. But I still wonder sometimes what it would have been like being raised by my parents."

All Ronnie can do is look into his eyes with sadness. She doesn't dare show him any pity. That is the last thing he wants. He prides himself on having beaten the odds. He had a grandmother who engaged in illegal activities, but who made sure her grandson was going to have a better life. She listens as he continues.

"You know Ronnie, sometimes I get so angry and blame myself that mom died giving birth to me and dad took off afterwards."

"It wasn't your fault, Preston."

"That's what grandma use to say. She would always try to comfort me, when she was hurting inside. She never got over mom's death, and she hated my father for abandoning me. Even though she felt sorry for me, I know she was glad that dad never tried to stay in contact. I can't even tell you what he looks like, Ronnie. Grandma got rid of all of his pictures. But pictures of my mom, her precious daughter, were all over the house. I even carry a picture of her in my wallet. My grandma couldn't get over losing her only daughter, and in the end I think that's what killed her. A broken heart. Anyway," he says, taking in a deep breath. "I have all the family I need in you."

"My wonderful man," she responds, with a warm and loving smile. "I don't know what I would do without you in my life."

"Well I'm going to make damn sure you never find out," he answers, kissing the tip of her nose. "I say, let's do what people in love do, and forget about everyone's problems, including Michael and Alex. What do you say?"

"I say bring it on, Big Daddy."

"Now who could this be knocking at this time of night?" Alex asks, slipping on a robe and stumbling towards the door. "Who is it?"

"It's Michael, let me in," a tired voice says.

Alex becomes quiet and stands by the door contemplating whether she should open it or not.

"Please Alex, open the door."

Slowly the door opens and Michael steps in.

"Michael, it's late. What are you doing here?"

"I had to see you, Alex, and plead with you again to come home."

"Listen to yourself, Michael. Begging does not become you, and I'm not at all impressed," she says walking over to the sofa. "Besides, why would I come home to a man who doesn't know the meaning of honesty?"

"Sweetheart, I can't divulge any information, not even to you. I promise you, I'll tell you everything in time."

"Michael!" she screams as she turns around to face him. "Come off of it, will you! Acting as if this is some kind of top secret. Well, it's no secret anymore. You lied and deceived me, and got caught. Now you expect me to accept it and we continue our life as if nothing's happened. I can't do that Michael. It's too painful."

Alex slowly eases down onto the sofa, places her hands over her face, and sobs. Michael walks over to her and sits next to her, then places his arm around her shoulder and draws her to him without resistance.

"Forgive me Alex?" he asks. "The last thing I want is to hurt you."

"Then why did you do it, Michael? I loved you."

Gently releasing her, Michael looks straight into her eyes. "Loved me? Don't you love me anymore, Alex?"

There's no answer. Alex only looks away.

"How can you turn your feelings off like that?" he asks.

Regaining her composure, she stands up and moves away from Michael. "Don't be foolish. You know I just can't stop loving you like that," she says, snapping her fingers.

"Then pack your things and come home. You can sleep in one of the guest rooms."

"Not tonight, Michael. I'm too tired to think. I'll give it some thought tomorrow. Right now I need a good night rest."

"Okay Alex," he responds, disappointed. "We'll do this your way. I know I've been pushy, and I'm sorry. I'll give you the time you need to ponder over what you should do. It hurts, you know, that you doubt me. But I guess I've given you a lot of reasons to. Until you hear the truth, our marriage won't survive. If you don't believe anything else, please believe me when I say you are my life, and I feel like I can't breathe without you."

Before she can say anything he's out the door. Alex goes into the bedroom in a daze and flops down on the bed. "Well, Les," she says out loud, "my efforts to deal with this situation failed. You felt I should be down in the dumps like you. Well, my sister, you got your wish." Alex then closes her watering eyes.

"What happened to me last night?" Les asks herself, holding her head and trying to sit up in bed. "How many drinks did I have? My head is pounding. And how did I get home?"

She slowly gets out of bed, fully clothed, and walks over to the mirror. And screams! The woman looking back at her is unrecognizable. Makeup smeared over her face, bags under her eyes, clothes wrinkled, hair tangled all over her head. "You look like a drunken slut!" she says out loud, and slowly walks into the bathroom.

Feeling a little refreshed after taking a shower, Les decides to work on her hair when the phone rang. "Hello," she answers, squinting her eyes from the pain shooting through her head. The ring of the phone had made her head hurt worse.

"Hi Les, it's Steve. Are you busy?"

"No, not at the moment," she answers.

"I'd like to stop by in about an hour, if it's okay with you."

"Did you forget something, Steve?" she asked, ignoring his question.

"No. We need to talk."

"What about, Steve? I thought we did that already."

"There's something else we need to discuss, Les. Please don't make this difficult."

"Personally, I don't think there's anything else to discuss at this point. But if you insist, okay. See you in an hour."

After hanging up the phone, she pace the floor. "What does he wants now!" she screams. "This is not the day for any deep discussions. I'm not in the mood.

If it wasn't for him, I wouldn't have made a fool out of myself in the first place," she says as she walks over to the window.

Looking out the window, she notices her car is missing. "What the hell!" she screams. "Where's my car? Someone stole my car," she says turning in circles, not knowing what to do next. "I know, I need to call the police. Oh God, this can't be happening to me."

When she reaches the phone, she suddenly stops. "Wait a minute," she says, loudly slapping her forehead. "I remember getting into a long white car. It must have been a limo. It was a limo, and the only person who could afford a limo in our family is Alex. No wonder I woke up in my clothes. Well, at least they took off my shoes." She smiles. "I guess I should call Alex to see if she can pick me up to get my car."

As Les reached for the phone, it ring. "Hello," she answers.

"Hi Les, how do you feel today?"

"Hey Alex, I was just getting ready to call you. Thanks for dropping me off last night."

"No problem. It was the least I could do. You really tied one on last night. So much out of character for you, Les."

"Yeah, well my whole life has taken a turn. What awaits me around the corner is unbeknownst to me."

"It seem like all our lives have taken on a transformation," Alex commented. "Some good and some bad. We can turn the bad into something positive. It's up to us, Les."

"You're right, but I guess I can't see how right now," she responds. "Maybe down the road things will become more clear to me. Then I can make rational decisions. Anyway, I was going to call you because I need a ride to pick up my car."

"That's no problem. I'll swing by in about a half hour and pick you up. Maybe we can have lunch."

"You're gonna have to make that about a couple of hours. Steve called this morning and wants to stop by and talk."

"Is that right?" Alex is curious now. "Did he say what about?"

"No he didn't. He wants to come over to discuss it."

"Whatever he has to say, you can handle it, Les. If he wants to come back home, that would be great."

"I'm not sure how great it is if we haven't solved our problems."

"Look at it this way, it's a start."

"Maybe it is, or maybe it's the end. Either way, I'll know soon. By the time you pick me up, I should know something, good or bad. See you in a couple of hours."

"Okay Les, good luck."

After hanging up the phone, Les walks over to her closet. Maybe Alex is right, she says to herself. What if he wants to come home? I should put on something nice for him. Nah, forget it. I'll throw on a pair of jeans and a sweatshirt. Why should I look nice for a man who dumped me?

While slipping on her jeans, the doorbell rings. He's early, she thinks, running into the bathroom to brush her hair. No time for looking cute, a ponytail will have to do. The doorbell rings again. She runs out of the bathroom, puts on her sweatshirt, then runs downstairs to open the door.

"You're early," she says, breathing hard.

"I know," he responds, walking into the house.

"Whatever you have to say must be very important for you to rush over."

"How are you?" he asks.

"I'm okay, considering. There's no change since you saw me yesterday. Okay, enough with the small talk," she says, being curt. "Let's cut to the chase. Why are you here, and what do you want?"

"We should go into the family room to discuss this," he says, taking hold of her arm. Les snatches it away and walks ahead. Steve holds his head down and follows.

Calm down Les, she says to herself, with anxiety building. Fear of what Steve is about to say and a lingering hangover are almost too much to bear.

Les sits in her favorite chair by the fireplace, and Steve sits in front of her on the ottoman. He takes her hands into his while staring into her eyes. Les stares back, trying to hold back her tears. At this point, her heart is about to jump out of her chest.

"Les, what I'm about to say doesn't come easy. Our life together, for the most part, has been wonderful. And I wouldn't have traded it for anything in this world. What we've shared, I will treasure for the rest of my life."

"Steve, what are you saying?" Now she's terrified.

"Please let me finish, okay?"

She nods.

He swallows hard. "These last past months have been hell on you, and I take full responsibility. But it's been hell on me too. For a long time I've been fighting certain feelings. They go back to my high school days.

I've never acted on those feelings to this very day, but they're real and I can't ignore them any longer."

Slowly, Les eases her hands away from his.

"Please don't pull away, Les. I need to explain this to you."

"What is there to explain!" she screams, then hauls off and slaps him. Getting up to move away, she continues. "I'm not naïve, you know. Just because I've been shut off from the world being a housewife, doesn't mean I don't know what's going on in it. The many times you made love to me, you were fantasizing about being with a man!"

"No, Les," he says, with tears in his eyes. "When I made love to you, it was real. My heart and mind was only with you."

"I can't believe this!" she screams. "I need to take an AIDS test, all because of you," she says, now pacing with her hand on her head.

"I told you, I didn't act on my feelings."

"How do I know you're telling me the truth, Steve? You've lied throughout our whole marriage."

"I swear Les, I have never been unfaithful," he says, now standing to reach out to her. She swings around to face him with coldness in her eyes.

"And I thought you were sick," she spits. "I went to see Dr. Richards to try to get him to tell me what was wrong with you."

"What made you think something was wrong?" he asks with a puzzled look.

"You were hiding your doctor appointments from me, and acting strange. How was I to know you're sick mentally and not physically?"

"I guess I deserve that," he says, turning away to walk back over to the ottoman to sit down. "However, I'm not mental."

Before he can finish she continues talking as if not hearing him. "And I was actually thinking of not opening my business because you might have been sick. I started feeling I was becoming selfish and neglecting my marriage. I almost made one of the biggest mistakes of my life."

As Les is venting, Steve doesn't interrupt. He knows she needs to get everything out, after destroying all hopes of them ever getting back together.

"Are you interested in a man?" she asks harshly.

"What? No!" he snaps.

"Don't you dare snap at me, Steve, acting like you're insulted. It's not like you don't swing both ways."

"Les I need to explore these feelings."

"And what if it's not what you really want, Steve? What are you going to do? Because you can't come back here!"

"Life goes on," he answers, holding his head down and fumbling with his keys.

"I need to know something, Steve."

"What?" he asks, lifting his head up.

"I caught you on the internet watching porn. But it was women, not men, you were watching. Can you explain that?" she asks, out of curiosity.

"At the time I was fighting my feelings, trying to make myself desire women. I even talked to Dr. Richards about what was going on. I asked him to refer me to a psychiatrist, which he did. That's what the appointment was about. I was going through my own personal hell. If only I had owned up to my feelings instead of ignoring them, I could have saved us both a lot of pain. Seeing a psychiatrist helped more than I thought it would. To the realization that it was time for me to make a decision. Last night I was pondering over whether I should lock all my feelings up and put them in a closet and come back home. Or come straight with you and put us both out of our miseries."

"I don't have to ask which decision you made," she says sarcastically.

"Les, we've both changed. We don't want the same things any longer. You know this as well as I do. We're at a dead end."

"I realize we've both changed, but I thought we could learn to accept the changes and continue to grow together. But you're right Steve," she agrees, with less anger in her voice. "There's nowhere for us to go but our separate ways. The anger will eventually leave, but then the thought of not having my husband here anymore will set in."

"You have your family to help you through this, Les. And I'm going to help by going away. We both need to start a new life. And for me, I'd rather go where no one knows me."

Visibly shaken, Les nods her head in agreement. Steve walks over to comfort her, but she moves away.

"Why wasn't my love good enough for you to bury those feelings?" she asks softly.

"We're only torturing ourselves by continuing to try and analyze this," he responds. "Accept it, Les, I have. The sooner you accept it, the sooner we can face each other without the hurt and pain."

"When are you leaving, and where are you going?" she asks, wiping tears away.

"I'm leaving next week for San Francisco," he answers.

"Oh, I should have known," she responds. "That's where gay people go, isn't it?"

Ignoring her comment, he continues. "Remember my buddy Craig?"

"Yes, I remember him. What about him?"

"He lives in San Francisco now, and he started his own business. When he first moved he wanted me to come there as a partner. I knew you wouldn't want to move, and plus I was waiting for my retirement, so I declined. I called him last night and asked if the offer still stood. He told me that he has a partner, but he could use another good electrician."

"So everything is falling into place for you, isn't it Steve?

"And for you too, Les. You're getting ready to start your own business. Something you've wanted for a very long time. Look, this is not what I had in mind when we married. I wanted us to grow old together, not apart. As far as the kids are concerned, I feel it's my responsibility to talk to them about what's going on, and hope they'll understand. I won't put that on you."

"How generous of you," she snaps. "I only hope you break it to them gently."

"I'm not going to tell them everything right away," he responds. Only that we're no longer together. When the time is right, I'll tell them the rest. And that's after you and I have had a chance to absorb everything. When it's all said and done, I hope we can be friends."

153

"Unlike you, Steve, I can't think that far ahead. Right now, I look at you and think disgust. At this point, the only conversation I want to have with you is about finances. We need to go to the bank before you leave."

"No matter how you feel about me right now, Les, remember I've always been a good husband and father. I know your judgment of me right now is cloudy, but I've always done the right thing. And I'll continue to do so. The house is yours. I already paid it off."

"So I guess guilt is eating you up alive, or else you're making sure I won't try to take you to the bank."

"Sure, guilt is part of it, but love is the other part, Les. I'm not a dog. We've been through a lot together. Raised beautiful and successful children. Because I'm going to find myself, doesn't mean I didn't love you. I still do Les, and I always will."

"That's all well and good Steve. And I thank you for caring enough and not just walking away. But I want you to understand that I'm going to call Michael. We need to go over our account together. Also I'm going to ask Michael to start divorce proceedings. There's no sense in trying to hold on to the past. So when you're settled, please send me your address."

"Don't worry, I will," he answers, impressed at the way Les is taking charge of her life already. "I guess I should leave now," he says, standing.

"Yes I agree," she says. "Alex is on her way, and she should be here soon."

"Hopefully we can meet with Michael by the middle of next week," he says, walking towards the door.

"I'll make sure that happens," she responds, rushing him out. "Goodbye, Steve."

Before he knows it, he's facing a closed door. Steve stands there for a second taking in all of the memories, knowing he will never return. He then turns and walks away.

After shutting the door, Les runs into the bathroom to throw up. Looking into the mirror after splashing cold water on her face, she sees a person both saddened and relieved. But what doesn't show is what she feels internally. The fear of a new beginning.

Belinda Walker-Graham

CHAPTER NINE

"I love how you move to the music as you clean," Preston says, sneaking up on Ronnie and grabbing her around the waist.

"You scared me, and stop nibbling on my neck unless you want me to take you right here."

"Take me baby," he commands.

Ronnie chuckles and slaps him playfully on the arm.

"Why are you so busy cleaning anyway?" he asks. "You cleaned this place from top to bottom the other day."

"You know how I am, Preston," she answers. "Whenever we're expecting company, I clean."

"And who, may I ask, are we expecting?"

"Only Alex," she answers, smiling. "She's stopping by on her way to pick up Les."

"Wait a minute. Only stopping by! Is that what I heard you say, Ronnie? All this work for only a few minutes. That does it! I'm taking you to CA."

"What's CA, baby?" she asked laughing?

Cleaners Anonymous," he answers. "You need help!" They both start laughing.

"Isn't that the buzzer I hear?" Ronnie asks.

"Yep, and I'll get it since your hands are full," he answers, patting her butt.

After hitting the buzzer, he stands at the door. When he hears footsteps getting close, he opens the door to Alex, holding an armful of magazines.

"Let me help you with those?" he asks.

157

"Thanks Preston," she says, handing over the magazines.

"I guess you ladies are going to have fun looking through these bridal magazines."

"Not for long," Ronnie answers as she approaches and takes the magazines. "Alex is leaving shortly to pick up the drunk in the family."

"You know Les would have a fit if she heard you," Alex says, laughing.

"I know," Ronnie says smugly. "Remind me to say it to her face the next time we're together."

"Don't think I won't," Alex responds. "I'm going to make sure I have a ringside seat!"

"I'm outta here baby," Preston says, giving her a juicy kiss. He then heads out the door.

"See ya," she says, blowing him a kiss.

"You two are so sickening, with all this lovey-dovey crap," Alex says.

"Oh, come on Alex. You and Michael had your share of mushy stuff."

"Yes we did," she responds with a smile. Then the smile faded. "That was once upon a time," she says, biting her lower lip. "Let's get into these magazines. I only have a few minutes before I have to leave to pick up Les."

"I'm surprised that Les waited this long to get her car," Ronnie comments.

"It wasn't by choice, believe me," Alex states. "Steve called wanting to meet with her."

"About what?"

"I don't know, Ronnie. He didn't want to discuss it over the phone."

"Goodness, look at the time," Alex says, looking down at her watch. "I have to get out of here."

"Okay," Ronnie replied. "I know you have to get Les. We can go over this another time. Thanks for bringing the magazines."

"No problem. I'll call you later."

Ronnie walks Alex to the door and gives her a hug. After closing the door, she walks back to the couch to look at the bridal magazines. While selecting the one she wants to look at, she notices a large manila envelope. What's this? she asks herself. Alex must have mixed this in with the magazines. These must be the photos Preston took, she thinks, walking over to the phone.

As she picks up the phone, she's thinking about how upset Alex is going to be when she notices the envelope missing.

"Hey Les, what's going on?"

"Oh, hi, Ronnie," Les answers somberly. "Nothing going on, why do you ask? Don't answer, I know. Alex told you Steve was coming over, didn't she?"

"Well, yes," Ronnie answers, confused. "But that's not why I called.

"Sorry Ronnie. I'm having a bad day."

"You want to talk about it?"

"No, not right now. All I want to do is get my car. I hope Alex gets here soon."

"She should be there shortly. She was here not too long ago to drop off some bridal magazines, and left her envelope on the table. It was mixed in with the magazines. That's the reason I called."

"I'll tell her whenever she gets here."

"Okay, Les, thanks. And call me if you need me."

"I will, talk to you later, Ronnie."

"That was strange," Ronnie says out loud, still holding the phone. "Steve must have really laid one on her."

After placing the phone down, Ronnie walks over to grab the envelope to put it aside for Alex. Without realizing it she picks it up upside down, and the contents fall out.

Bending down to pick up the pictures, Ronnie gasps and covers her mouth in shock. Pictures of Michael and the woman are staring her in the face. "This can't be," she says. "I don't believe this."

"Don't believe what?" Preston asks, walking just then back through the door, returning to pick up his cell phone. Looking at Ronnie, he can tell something is wrong. She's speechless.

"Baby, what's wrong?" he asks, concerned.

"Look at this, Preston," she says, getting up off the floor to hand him the pictures.

"I've already seen these, Ronnie. Remember, I took them. Anyway, how did you get hold of these?"

"Alex left them on the table. When I reached for the envelope to put them away, all the contents fell out."

"Like I said, I've already seen them, so let's put the pictures back in the envelope."

"Preston, you don't understand," she says, pleading for him to listen. "This woman, here in the picture, is the same woman Paris fought at the restaurant!"

"Baby, you're not saying what I think you're saying?" Now he was very interested.

"Oh, I have your full attention now, don't I? To answer your question, yes. That's the same tramp Neil slept with."

"Well I'll be," he responds. "This mystery woman is quite busy."

"Yeah, busy bed-hopping with my brother-in-laws. I wonder if she's made her way to Steve's bed."

"Why you say that?"

"Because he's acting strange, and nobody knows why," she comments.

"You don't know why, because it's none of your business," he says in a stern voice. "Furthermore, we don't know what's actually going on between Michael and this woman."

"I do know this much, Preston. That woman is trouble. I can feel it."

"I agree with you on that one," he responds, nodding his head. "When I went to Chicago, I was approached by two FBI agents. They told me to stay clear of their case, and took my film. Evidently, there's more to this story than just horny folks. I think I'm going to make a call to a buddy of mine. He's privileged to information that I'm not. Maybe he can shed some light on what's going on."

"I hope so Preston, before someone gets hurt. And I don't want it to be any of my sisters. I'm sure neither Alex nor Paris have any idea their husbands are dealing with the same woman."

"And you're going to make sure they don't know, right?" he demands.

"I can't make any promises, Preston. I love you, and most of the time I agree with you. But this time it's different. My sisters are involved in something very serious. I can't just ignore this."

"Well, if you must tell them, fine," he concedes. "But please leave out the FBI part until I get more information."

"Okay, I promise not to divulge any info about the FBI," she says as she sits on the sofa.

"Look at you, Ronnie. You can't wait to talk to your sisters, can you?"

"What are you talking about?" she asks, agitated.

"You can't sit still, your legs are shaking. That's what I'm talking about." He walks over to sit next to her, then places his hand on her legs. "It's going to be okay, baby," he says, trying to comfort her. "I know you're worried about your sisters."

"Preston," she says, turning to look at him. "When I left Atlanta, I was jumping for joy. Coming home to my man and family was all I could think about for months. Little did I know what I was really coming home to. We're simple folks, living simple lives. How could all this be happening? We're getting older. Things are supposed to fall in place, you know, get better."

"Baby, everything is falling into place," he responds, rubbing her close-cropped hair. "We're getting married, and you have a job offer. You're jumping right into a new and wonderful life. Everything will turn out fine for your sisters, too."

Ronnie reaches over to give Preston a hug. "You're so good for me," she whispers in his ear.

"We're good for each other," he whispers back, pretending as if she's choking him.

"Okay you faker," she says, releasing him with a smile.

"Now that you seems to be okay, Big Daddy has to go into the office," he says, kissing the tip of her nose. "I need to make some calls. Are you sure you're okay?" he asks, taking on a serious look.

"Go," she answers, pushing him off the sofa. "I'm fine, baby."

"If you say so, but I know my baby," he comments. "You may have calmed down some, but it's still on your mind. I'm going to head out now, but I won't be long," he says, getting up to leave. "Maybe we can go to that new jazz club just opened downtown Detroit this evening. What do you think?"

"We'll see," is all she can say as she gets up to walk him to the door.

"I promise to hurry back baby," he says, not wanting to leave her.

"Okay," she responds, managing a smile. He kisses her on the cheek and leaves.

"Oh God," she says out loud. Then she thinks, What a mess. I need to figure out how to break this to Alex and Paris. Alex is so fragile right now, and Paris is too, even though she tries to hide it. This is driving me crazy. A cigarette is what I need right now to calm down.

Shaking her head, she walks over to the table and grabs her keys. I better take a walk instead, she says to herself. I can't break my promise I made to Preston. He'd be so disappointed. Anyway, walking will clear my head on how I'm going to deal with Paris. She's such a handful. After my walk I'll give her a call.

163

Convincing her to come over is the easy part. The hard part is keeping them both under control.

Especially Paris, she says to herself, thinking back on the incident the night before. She shakes her head in disbelief and walks out the door.

"Neil, there are two men at the door saying they're with the FBI," Paris whispers nervously.

Neil stares at her, puzzled. "FBI?" he asks, with a curious look on his face. "Are you sure?"

"Yes, I'm sure," she answers, still whispering.

"What do they want?" he asks, trying to speak low.

"How am I supposed to know?" she responds, looking back at the door. "Why are you asking questions? Are you guilty of something I don't know about?"

"Of course not, Paris!" he yells, then suddenly lowers his voice.

"Well, go see what they want," she says, pushing him towards the door and walking behind him at the same time.

Neil opens the door. "What can I do for you gentlemen?" he asks.

"Are you Neil Findley?" one of the men asks.

"Yes I am."

"I'm Agent Farley, and this is Agent Moss," the man says, holding up his ID. "May we step inside, sir?"

"What is this all about?" Neil demands, trying to take control.

"We prefer to discuss this matter inside, sir," Agent Moss answers.

"Well, alright," Neil says reluctantly. "I hope this doesn't take too long. My boys will be home soon."

"Excuse us ma'am," Agent Farley says as he walks past Paris, followed by Agent Moss.

"This way gentlemen," Neil instructs as he points in the direction of the family room. He motions them to sit. "Now why do you need to talk to me?

"Mr. Findley, I'm going to get straight to the point," Farley says. "We're investigating a woman by the name of Marlene Sims. Does that name ring a bell with you?"

Shocked, Neil nods yes.

"What does your investigation have to do with my husband?" Paris asks, looking directly at Farley, noticing an ugly scar by his ear.

"We know your husband had an affair with this woman at one time," he answers. "We also know you're aware of the affair."

Both Neil and Paris look at each other with confused faces.

Moss speaks up. "We've been investigating this woman for a very long time. Which means we know her every move, and yours as well, if you were around her."

"What are you investigating her for?" Neil asks.

"Ms. Sims has been smuggling drugs in and out of the country for some time now," Farley says.

"I wasn't aware of that, nor did I have anything to do with it," Neil states nervously.

"Mr. Findley, we're aware of that," Moss assures him. "You were also investigated. Since you're a pilot, we didn't know what connections you had with Ms. Sims, or the person she's working for."

Neil stands up, rubbing his head, and starts pacing. "I don't understand, Agent Moss," he says, confused. "Since you have everyone under surveillance, you should know Marlene and I are no longer involved."

"We also know, Mr.Findley, that Ms. Sims has contacted you once recently, and at your home several times," Moss answers. "Ms. Sims also had a run-in with your wife a second time, may I add. You both need to stay as far away from Ms. Sims as possible. We're too close to cracking this case, and we don't need any interference."

"That's right," Farley agrees. "We don't want anyone jeopardizing the long hard work we put into building this case. I hope you heed our warning and stay clear of this woman. We don't want anyone to get hurt. Ms. Sims deals with very dangerous people. In fact, she can be quite dangerous herself if provoked."

"Is there anything else we need to know?" Paris asks, giving them the cue to leave.

"Yes, keep a close watch on your boys," Farley suggests.

Both Neil and Paris look at each other with fear in their eyes.

"Is that all gentlemen?" Neil asks.

"For now, yes," Moss answers as they stand, finally taking the hint.

Paris sits frozen while Neil escorts both men out. When they reach the door Farley pulls out a card. "This is where you can reach us," he says, handing it to Neil.

"Don't hesitate to use it," Moss says as they turn to walk away.

Neil stands in the door for a second looking down at the card, then shuts the door.

Neither Neil or the two agents notice the woman in the blue Lexus parked across the street.

Marlene watches as the agents enter their vehicle and pull off. "Something's going on," she says suspiciously. "I guess that's my cue to back off of Miss Paris and Neil right now. My first priority is completing this deal. But when it's over, I'll be back." She starts her car. "So for right now, count your lucky stars, bitch." Marlene stares at the house for a second, smiles mischievously, then pulls off.

When Neil walks into the room, Paris jumps up. "See!" she screams, pointing her finger at Neil. "That's what happens when you're out there doing wrong. You put this family in jeopardy because you couldn't keep that thing in your pants. If it wasn't for the fact that me and the boys are involved in the mess, I'd say it serves you right!"

"So much for forgiveness," Neil responds.

"Okay, I'm sorry for screaming," she says, with little real remorse. "But when I forgave you, we were going to put the past behind us and move on. How can we move on when that nut is still in our lives, and possibly planning to harm us?"

"I'd give my life to protect my family," he answers with force. Giving in to her fear, Paris walks into Neil's arms for comfort.

Releasing himself from her embrace, he takes her hand and walks over to the sofa. "Paris," he says, still holding her hand, "I think we should let the boys stay with my mother until all this blows over." Before she can speak, he continues. "I know you'd feel better if

167

they were here with us. But I feel they'll be safer with mom."

"If you strongly believe the boys will be safer at your mother's, then I won't object," she says with sincerity. "But how are we going to explain it to Brian and Brandon? They're so bright, Neil. I'm afraid they're going to suspect something's wrong."

"Only if we don't explain it convincingly to them," he answers. "We can tell them we're really concerned about their grandmother staying in that big house all alone. And because we both will be pulling in a lot of overtime at our jobs, it's best they stay with her. Remember, Paris, we're the parents. We need to let them know how much we love them, and that we feel this is the best solution. Plus mom is only a few minutes away. It's not like they're going to another state. I'm sure they'll understand," he says, pulling her close to him. "However, I do worry about mom getting involved in this mess. We'll have to fill her in. She needs to know and not be in the dark, in case something happens."

Paris nods her head in agreement, then looks up into Neil's eyes. "You know, in my heart I believed you. I was just so upset that this woman was back in our lives, and angry at you for putting her in our lives in the first place. I'm sorry Neil."

"Sweetheart, you have nothing to be sorry about. I caused this mess by doing what I did. By not being man enough to deal with our problems. Instead I tried to escape, which was wrong and caused more problems. I'm the one who should be begging your forgiveness. After this is over, I'm going to be the kind of husband and father that both you and the boys can be proud of."

"Oh Neil, I love you so much."

"I love you too," he says, and kisses her passionately. "I can kiss you all night, among other things," he says after their lips part.

"Unfortunately, we can't get too carried away. Brandon and Brian should be arriving home shortly."

"Well, in that case, I'm going upstairs to take a cold shower," he responds, jumping up and shaking his pants loose.

"While you're taking a shower, I'm going to give Ronnie a call. She called and left a message for me to call her. She sound a little out of breath."

"Maybe she and Preston just finished what we were trying to start," he says, rubbing up against her.

"Go take that cold shower," she says, giggling. "I have a call to make."

Paris watches as Neil stubbornly walks away to go upstairs. "What a stud," she says with a smile on her face. Then she picks up the phone to call Ronnie.

"Hello," the voice on the other end answers.

"What'ca doing sis?"

"Waiting on Alex to stop back over," Ronnie says.

"I got your message. You sounded like you were out of breath. What were you doing?"

"I went out for a walk," Ronnie answers.

"I don't believe it!" Paris exclaims. "Not 'Miss I don't need exercise to stay looking good.'"

"Believe it. I thought I could use a breath of fresh air. Anyway, are you up to driving over here tonight?"

"I guess. What's happening tonight?"

"Nothing, really. Since Alex is coming over, I thought maybe we all can get together, sit around and talk."

"Let me talk to Neil first. He may have made plans for us this evening. If he has, I'll call you back, otherwise I'll see you in about an hour."

"See you in an hour I hope," Ronnie responds, and hangs up.

"Neil, sweetheart!" Paris yells.

"What is it?" he answers, walking out of the bedroom into the hallway with a towel wrapped around his waist. Paris walks to the bottom of the stairs so he can hear her better. Looking up at him with that towel around his waist, and seeing his sculptured body, makes her lose her train of thought. "Um," she says, trying to gather her thoughts, "oh, I wanted to know if you have plans for us tonight."

"No, not really, why?"

"Because I want to run by Ronnie's for about an hour or two."

"Honey, I have no plans for us tonight. But after our surprise visit today, I don't think it's wise for you to go out alone."

"Neil, we can't run scared. I'm not going to let that tramp dictate our every move. And you shouldn't, either."

"If it was only me to be concerned about, I'd agree. But with you and the boys involved, I don't want to take any chances. Nor do I want you to take any chances, Paris."

"I'll be very careful," she says, trying to reassure him. "I promise, Neil."

"On one condition, Paris. You make sure you call when you get there, and when you're getting ready to walk out that door to come home."

"Yes sir," she answers with a salute. "Give the boys a kiss for me, and tell them I'll see them later tonight."

"What about daddy?" he asks, smiling, as he walks down the stairs. "Do I get a kiss?"

"Oh yeah," she says in a sexy voice, as she snatches off his towel, then gives him a long kiss.

"Mm, are you sure you want to go over to Ronnie's?" he moans.

"I'm sure. Oh, and sweetheart, it looks as if you need that cold shower," she says, laughing, and walks out the door.

All the way to Ronnie's apartment Paris is paranoid, looking around and constantly glancing into her rear view mirror. This is ridiculous, she thinks, pulling into the apartment complex. I'm not going to live like this. After parking the car, she jumps out and runs to the building. So much for not letting that tramp dictate my life, she thinks while pressing the buzzer. By the time she reaches the apartment door she's out of breath. "I've got to start working out again," she says aloud.

While she bends over with her hands on her hips, trying to catch her breath, the door opens.

"What's wrong with you?" Ronnie asks with a worried look. "I heard you running down the hall like a crazed woman."

"If you only knew," Paris says, pushing past Ronnie to enter the apartment. "I thought I saw Alex's car outside. Is she here?"

171

"Yep, she's in the bathroom. It seems like she's been in there for an half hour."

"What's she doing in there?" Paris whispers.

"I don't know, Paris, probably primping. You know how she likes to look at herself in the mirror."

"Are you two cows talking about me behind my back?" Alex asks, strutting out of the bathroom.

"You look quite fresh, Alex," Paris comments. "Who are you trying to impress? There are no men here. And we definitely don't care how you look. Remember, we grew up with you."

"Shut up, Paris," she snaps. "I like looking good all the time, you know that."

"And you like being uppity, too," Ronnie adds. "Look at you Alex. And why are you wearing stiletto heels? We're not going out to party."

"I like showing off my gorgeous legs, that's why," she answers, strutting over to the sofa.

"You're incorrigible," Paris comments. "Anyway, where's Les?"

"She's out of it," Alex answers. "Steve was over there earlier today. Whatever he said really bummed her out. She didn't talk the whole time we were in the car."

"Wow, I wonder what Steve told her?" Ronnie says, intrigued.

"I invited her to ride over with me, but she declined," Alex states.

"Maybe we should go over and try to cheer her up," Paris comments.

"Yeah, like you tried to do for me, by all of us going out to dinner, right," Alex says smugly. "Which turned into a fiasco, may I add."

"That was Paris acting a fool," Ronnie pipes in.

"Les wasn't an angel, you know, Paris retorts.

"In defense of Les," Alex says, getting up and walking towards the kitchen, "she was in pain from her marriage falling apart. And I know how that feels. She needs time to think right now."

"We all know how it feels to have our marriage fall apart," Ronnie says. "But you're right, Alex. Les does need time to absorb the change in her life. Hopefully they can resolve their problems, and get their marriage back on track. And now that I've had my say, I've become thirsty. Alex, pour me a glass of wine, will you?"

"Goodness Ronnie, you didn't make a speech, only a comment," Paris states. "I know that little comment didn't make you thirsty. And by the way, pour me a glass too Alex."

"Who do you all think I am?" Alex asks. "I'm not even the host. Ronnie should have her butt in here serving us!"

Just as Paris is walking over to pour her own glass of wine, the buzzer rings.

"Now who could that be?" Ronnie asks. "I'm not expecting any more company."

"Go ask who it is, girl," Alex commands. "I'm pouring the wine."

"I'll see who it is," Paris says, getting up. At the intercom she asks, "Who is it?"

"It's me, Les," the voice outside says.

They all look at each other with puzzled faces. The buzzer rings again.

"Let her in, Paris," Ronnie says with insistence.

"So 'Miss never need anyone' shows up for comfort after all," Alex comments, walking back into the living room with two glasses.

"What's wrong with you?" Ronnie asks, taking her glass of wine. "At first you're sympathizing with Les, now you're making snide remarks. No more wine for you tonight Alex."

"It's not the wine, she's just evil," Paris says.

"Hush," Ronnie says to Paris. "I hear her coming. We don't want her to think we're discussing her."

"We are," Alex comments. "Open the door, so we can say it to her face."

Ronnie gives Alex the evil eye as she walks over to open the door. "Hey sis," she says. "You decided to stop by."

"Yep," Les answers as she walks through the door. "Alex must have told you that I wanted to stay home to have a pity party."

"You're right on the money," Ronnie replies. "But I'm glad you changed your mind. It wouldn't have been the same without you. We all can have a pity party together."

"What do you have to be down and out about, Ronnie?" Alex asks. "Since you're getting married and all. You're suppose to be extremely happy, remember?"

"I think you better chill," Ronnie responds with a warning.

After that exchange, Les leans over to Paris and whispers, "Alex is in a foul mood, I see."

"Yeah, she is," Paris answers. "She should know after all these years, not to push Ronnie's buttons."

"What are you two sitting on the floor whispering about?" Alex asks.

"I have no problem repeating myself," Paris answers. "I said you should have learned by now not to push Ronnie's buttons. Especially after what she did to you the day mom and dad went to get our roller skates."

Ronnie starts laughing, remembering the day she stood up to Alex.

"Oh yeah," Les says, perking up. "We were doing our usual. Sitting on the porch talking about whoever walked down the street, when all of a sudden Alex demanded that Ronnie water the grass."

"You know, Les, I never understood why Alex was picking on Ronnie," Paris remarks.

"Me either," Les says. But she didn't pick on her any more after that."

"Are you all done reminiscing?" Alex asks, now irritated.

"No," Paris says, laughing. "We haven't finished yet. Go ahead Les, continue."

"I'll be happy to," Les says. "So Ronnie got up quietly, went to the side of the house, grabbed the hose as if she was going to water the grass, but watered Alex instead." Les is now laughing so hard she can't finish the story.

"And wait a minute," Paris says, holding up her hand and laughing hysterically. "Remember, Alex had just returned from getting her hair done for a date she had with that guy Carl."

"Now why would you bring that bum up?" Alex asks.

"You didn't think he was a bum then," Ronnie speaks up. "As I recall you loved his dirty draws."

"No, I loved what he had in them," Alex says, forcing a smile.

"Enough of Alex," Paris interrupts, turning to Les. "What's happening with you and Steve?"

"Lay off, Paris," Ronnie insists. "Let's talk about something more pleasant. Anyway, when Les is ready to talk about it she will."

"Wasn't it you who said we can have a pity party together?" Paris asks Ronnie. "You and Alex want to know as much as I do."

"I may have said that, Paris, but it's on a voluntary basis," Ronnie answers. "Les hasn't volunteered any information."

Paris turns to Les. "Come on now, Les," she begs. "You want to talk about it as much as we want to hear it, or else you wouldn't have come here."

Gathering her composure and taking a deep breath, Les begins. "As you all know through Alex, with her big mouth, Steve came by." She stops for a minute and sees all eyes on her. Everyone is completely silent. She continues. "Anyway, what he told me blew my mind, and I'm still in shock."

Unable to keep silent, Alex speaks up. "Probably had an affair."

"I wish that was the case," Les says. "But no, it was not an affair, it's worse. See, Steve wants to find himself."

"Don't they all," Alex comments. "They never know what they want."

"Shut up, Alex!" both Ronnie and Paris scream.

"We want to hear what Les has to say, not you," Ronnie says.

Paris looks over at Ronnie, not believing her ears. "I thought you weren't interested," she remarks. "You're just as nosey as the rest of us."

"Will you all let me finish?" Les insists. Everyone gets quiet again. "As I was saying, Steve wanted to find himself. But unfortunately it wasn't because he's getting older. That I could handle. He's having an identity crisis. Maybe that's putting it lightly. I should say a sexual identity crisis."

Looking around she notices everyone's expression. Paris's mouth flies open. Alex looks like a mannequin, with her drink halfway to her mouth. And Ronnie nearly chokes on the wine she has just taken a sip of.

"I can tell by your reactions that all of you picked up on the real reason Steve left," Les comments.

"How did he explain it to you?" Paris asks, still stunned.

"He said that he's been having certain feelings since high school, but never acted on them."

"I say he's lying!" Alex shouts. "He must have a lover. Why would he walk away from his marriage if he didn't?" she asks, talking louder.

"Lower your voice," Ronnie whispers. "I don't want the neighbors complaining. Now Les, he didn't have to tell you anything," she continues. "But when you think about it, he did you a favor."

"Is that what you think, Ronnie?" Les is shocked that Ronnie would make such a statement. "He's destroyed my faith in men. I wouldn't know if I'm with a real man or one who's perpetrating."

"That's all part of the dating scene," Paris comments. "You never know what their into, unless they tell you. Or by observing and then going with your gut feelings. That's why I always carried protection. I didn't know where that young boy laid his hat."

"God, I'm too old for this," Les sighs, looking up at the ceiling. "I'm suppose to be settled, happy with my husband. Not looking for my next piece of meat."

"Ah, get over it like I did," Alex slurs, spilling her drink while motioning with her hand.

"That's it," Ronnie says, snatching the glass out of her hand. "Your drinks are cut off! Furthermore, you're not over it. Sitting here drowning your sorrows. I'm going into the kitchen to put on a pot of coffee. I won't allow any of you to walk out this door highly intoxicated."

Alex looks at Ronnie speechless, then falls back onto the couch.

"Look at her," Paris says, pointing. "That's pitiful. She's so bitter. And she wants to bring Les down with her."

"You know what they say," Ronnie yells from the kitchen. "Misery loves company."

"Take a good look," Paris says, turning to Les. "I know you don't want to let your bitterness get to you like that. Remember how momma use to talk about Beulah Mae, the drunk?"

"Oh yeah," Les remembers with a smile. "She used to walk up and down the street in mismatched clothes, like she didn't know where she was going."

"She didn't," Ronnie yells again from the kitchen. "One day she walked past her own house. Momma shook her head and said that's a rotten shame. She looked at us and said that's how we'd turn out if we started drinking." Thinking back on the memory of her mother, Ronnie smiles to herself.

But Les is laughing hysterically, pointing at Alex. "That's Beulah Mae the drunk," she says. Paris joins in on the laughter.

"I heard that," Alex remarks, lifting up her head. "I still have my wits about me."

"You can't even stand up," Ronnie says as she walks into the living room with a cup of coffee in her hand. "Here, she says, handing Alex the cup. "Sit up and drink this, so you can function."

Struggling to an upright position, Alex takes the cup. "By the way," she says, "where's your husband-to-be?"

"He had to go into the office to check on something. Which reminds me, I have something for you."

"Oh, right, the envelope," Alex says, remembering. "I didn't even realize it was mixed in with the magazines. Maybe in my own way I was trying to get rid of it. I left some of the pictures at the house. That's how Michael knew about them. What I really need to do is burn them."

"Well, here they are," Ronnie says, handing Alex the envelope. "Now you can do whatever you want with them."

Alex reaches for the envelope with shaky hands, then places it close to her heart.

Trying to divert attention from Alex, Paris speaks up. "Neil and I had two surprise visitors today."

"Who, the twins?" Ronnie asks, laughing.

"No silly, they live there," Paris answers.

"You can't fool me," Les remarks. "They're at Neil's mom more than at their own home."

"She's lonely!" Paris exclaims. "Anyway, you'll never guess, so I'll tell you. It was the FBI."

Even Alex leaned forward to hear more.

"The F-B-I," Les says, spelling it out very slowly.

"Yes, I didn't stutter," Paris answers.

"Why would they want to talk to you?" Ronnie inquires.

"I'll give you one clue," Paris answers, holding up one finger. "Her name starts with an 'M' and I had to beat her down."

"That's two clues," Alex remarks.

"Anyway," Paris continues, ignoring Alex. "Apparently this woman is involved with the mob. She's been transporting drugs. And because Neil is a pilot, he's been under investigation since the beginning of the affair. Even though the affair is over, the FBI has been tapping the phone and following us. They knew about the fight we had, for God sake."

"How do you feel?" Les asks. "This is an invasion of your privacy."

"I'm angry as hell," she responds. "I swore to Neil, I wasn't going to change my routine because of that woman. But what did I do? I was so paranoid on the drive here. Constantly checking the rear view mirror to see if I was being followed. Then I ran from the car to the door. I was all out of breath by the time I reached the apartment. Neil seems to think the boys will be safer with his mom, out of harm's way."

"He's right, you know," Ronnie agrees, walking back into the kitchen, deciding against divulging her new-found information.

Looking back on her sisters from the open kitchen brings back wonderful memories of their childhood. How they would sit around in the family room discussing their dreams and goals. Little did we know the twist and turns we'd have to go through to try and get there, she says to herself, staring on. Suddenly a voice snaps her back to reality.

"Hey girl," Les says, standing up to walk towards the kitchen. "Whatever you're thinking about must be really good. Give me some of those thoughts."

"Trust me, you don't want them," Ronnie answers with a fake smile while wiping the counter down.

Les walks over to put her hand on Ronnie's shoulders. "What's wrong?" she asks, concerned.

"Look at you," Ronnie says sympathetically. "You're always the big sister, no matter what you're going through. Well, it's time for us to take care of you. I know this must be hard on you, Les. How are you, really?"

"Oh Ronnie, I don't know," she answers shrugging her shoulders. "I'm still in shock, I guess. Man or woman, to me he still had an affair."

"How so?"

"It may not have been physical," she tries to explain, "but it was definitely an affair of the heart. I guess that's what hurts so much. In his heart, he wants someone other than me. He just doesn't know who it is yet." She then looks into Ronnie's eyes with such sadness. It tears at Ronnie's heart to see her sister in all that pain.

181

"I'm mentally drained," Les continues. "It's time to call it a night."

"I agree," Ronnie says, understanding Les's need to be alone. She walks over to give Les a big sisterly hug.

"Have you shrunk?" Les asks, out of the blue.

Ronnie releases her embrace and steps back. Looking at Les, she bursts out laughing, and Les joins in.

"I've always been an inch shorter," Ronnie remarks, still laughing.

"You seem even shorter for some reason."

"Probably because I'm barefooted," Ronnie says. "I don't know how you segued into that, but I see you still have a sense of humor. And that's good, considering. Anyway, I'm going to walk you to the door, so you can go home while you have some energy left."

"Good idea," Les smiles.

They both walk out of the kitchen hugging and laughing, into a pair of staring eyes. "What was that all about?" Alex asks.

"Oh, nothing," Les smirks. "Where's Paris?"

"She's in the bedroom talking to Neil."

"Well, I'm outta here, guys," Les says, waving her hand.

"Talk to you tomorrow," Paris yells, walking out of the bedroom, noticing Les getting ready to leave.

After shutting the door, Ronnie walks over to the lazy boy and flops down. Paris sits on the sofa next to Alex, instead of the floor, to get more comfortable. All three look at each other, smile, then lay their heads back to chill.

"Hey Zack, what's up, man?" Preston asks over the phone.

"Crime, man," he answers. "What can I do for you, Pres? I know you didn't call for sweet talk."

"Sure didn't. I can get that at home. I need a favor, man."

"Shoot."

"I need you to run a check on a Marlene Sims. This lady has been quite busy, and I need to know what she's up to."

"You got it, Pres. Give me a couple of days."

"Thanks, man," Preston says and hangs up.

"Okay Miss Marlene," he says out loud, leaning back into his chair. "There's more to this story than just affairs, and I'm going to find out what."

Belinda Walker-Graham

CHAPTER TEN

"Why are you calling me on this number?" he asks angrily. "You have my private number. And how did you get this number anyway?"

"I have my sources," she answers. "You made a foolish mistake, Michael, by involving the FBI. Since you didn't heed my warning, plans have changed."

"What's the next move?" he asks, sounding defeated.

"That's more like it," she says, knowing she has the upper hand. "I like that tone better, and so will my boss. His patience is much shorter than mine. He was very angry with you, Michael. So angry that he flew into Michigan yesterday to meet with you."

"When?"

"I'll get back with you soon to give instructions," she answers, then hangs up. I know I should lay low, she says to herself, but I can't get that bitch Paris off my mind.

"Hey Marlene, get your ass in here and finish your job."

"I'm busy!" she yells back, irritated.

Before she knows it, he grabs her from behind and throws her against the wall. "When I say jump, you say how high," he says, with his hand around her throat. "Don't ever disobey me again!" He then releases her.

"I'm sorry baby," she says, rubbing her neck. "I was making that call for you. Just doing what you asked of me." She walks over to him and starts stroking his bald head.

"Who do you think you're trying to con, bitch?" he spits, pulling her head back by grabbing her hair.

"Please don't hurt me," she begs.

Ignoring her plea, he continues. "Do you actually think you can get over on me, by trying to sweet talk me? Because if you do," he says, pulling harder and listening to her scream, "you have another thing coming."

He releases her and watches as she falls to the floor. Smiling, he walks over to the bar. "Besides, you're not as good as you think. I've had better. I only keep you around because you're greedy, and you do have some brains.

"So what did Mr. Big Shot have to say for himself?" he asks while pouring his drink.

"He didn't deny telling the feds," she answers, rubbing her head.

"How did he react when you told him I wanted to meet?" he inquires, taking a sip of his drink.

"A little nervous. I told him we'll get back with him."

"Good," he says, smiling. "I want him to be nervous and afraid. As he should be. Now, come on my dear. It's time for you to get busy."

Walking behind him, heading towards the bedroom, Marlene gets nauseous. The thought of him all over her makes her sick to her stomach. I hate that bald headed bastard, she says to herself. After all these years, he still treats me like a whore. Well, it will be over soon. And little does he know, I'm getting as far away from him as I can.

When she reaches the bedroom she puts on her fake smile and begins the role she's about to play. As he sits on the bed, she gets down on her knees.

"Now do what whores are good at," he demands.

Marlene closes her eyes, wishing he was dead, and dreading the act she is about to perform.

"Show him up, Doris."

"Yes sir," she answers, then leaves.

That was fast, Michael says to himself as he walks over to his desk. Before he can sit down, there's a knock. "Come on in," he commands.

Preston walks through the door.

"I'm glad you could make it on such short notice," Michael says, standing up to greet him.

"What's happening, man?" Preston responds, extending his arm to shake Michael's hand.

"A whole lot, my friend," he answers, accepting his hand. He motions for Preston to take a seat and eases down into his own chair. "How's my sister-in-law?"

"She's doing just great," Preston answers. "From the look of things, I can't say the same for you. I can clearly see you're troubled. You look haggard. Like you haven't slept in days. What's going on?"

"You're a straight shooter, I see."

"Goes with the nature of my job," Preston says.

Getting up from his chair, Michael walks over to the window. Watching him very closely, Preston leans back into his chair and crosses his legs, thinking how difficult it must be for Michael to open up. He can't even face me, Preston says to himself.

Standing with his back towards Preston, Michael finally starts to speak. "There's a lot going on in my life right now." Turning to face Preston, he hesitates, then continues. "I'm being blackmailed by this woman. But she isn't working alone. There's some man who's calling all the shots. It's the same woman that Alex thinks I'm having an affair with."

Michael stops speaking to give Preston a chance to jump in. But Preston doesn't say a word. Through experience, he has learned not to interrupt when someone is opening up to him.

When Michael realizes Preston isn't going to speak, he continues. "They're asking for millions of dollars. I swear to you Preston, I didn't have an affair."

Preston finally speaks up. "I'm not the one to convince, Michael."

"Maybe not, but you took the pictures, and they're very incriminating. I don't want you to think I'm that kind of a man. I have my faults, but I'd never disrespect Alex like that. It's only natural that Alex would turn to you for help. But I wish you'd stayed out of it. Alex seeing those photos of me and Marlene has complicated things even more. I didn't want her involved."

"Then you should have handled your business better, or told Alex what was going on," Preston suggests. "But if this is what you wanted to see me about, then I'm outta here." He stands. "My job is done. You're on your own. I'd say the same for Alex, if it wasn't for the fact that she's Ronnie sister."

"Wait, Preston," Michael says, stepping away from the window. "The reason I called was to try and convince you to talk Alex into coming home."

"I think that's your job, my man."

"And how was I to do that without telling her the truth? So I came to the conclusion that after explaining my situation, you'll feel as I do. That Alex would be safer at home. She'd listen to you."

"Michael, I've been in this business a long time, and I can tell when someone's not coming clean with me. You're hiding something. And until you disclose all the information, don't look to me for help."

Michael walks over to his desk and takes a seat in his leather chair. He then places his hands over his face, not caring about showing his emotions. He sits there drowning in his self pity. Mother would be appalled if she saw me like this, he says to himself. She always believed showing emotions was a sign of weakness. He lifts his head up to see Preston sitting back down in the chair.

"I can't walk out on you like that, man," Preston says with sympathy. "I got into this business to help people. It seems to me that you're in serious trouble. And from the looks of it, you're trapped in a hole you can't get out of."

Preston then straightens up, looking Michael square in the face. "Why were the FBI following me?" he asks.

Finally realizing he needs someone to confide in, Michael speaks up. "They weren't following you, Preston," he says somberly. "It was me they were following. Or should I say, us."

"What do you mean, us?"

"Let me clarify this. When I say us, I mean myself and Marlene. They were initially trailing Marlene because of drug trafficking. You see, they suspect

Marlene of transporting drugs for this big-time drug lord named Shark."

Preston suddenly perks up and leaned forward.

"I guess you've heard of this Shark fellow," Michael says, noticing Preston's reaction.

"Oh yes I have. I first heard of him when I started on the police force. He's been around a long time, and he's very cunning. When the FBI finally caught up with this guy, they couldn't even make the charges stick. And I'm talking everything from murder to tax evasion. This cat knows how to beat the system."

"So you see Preston, it's imperative that Alex stay as far away from this mess as possible. You've got to convince her to return home where she'll be safe. Because I can't," he says, bewildered.

"I understand where you're coming from," Preston responds sympathetically. "Let's say I convince Alex to return home. What makes you think she'll be safe here? We're talking about crazed folks here. They won't think twice about snuffing you or Alex out. And they'll go to any lengths to do it."

"Don't you think I realize that?" Michael says with trepidation. "The thought of something happening to Alex petrifies me. That's why I took the step I did in hiring a bodyguard. I need someone to protect her since I can't."

"That was a smart move," Preston agrees. "Tell you what I'll do. Since this is a serious situation, I'll talk to Alex."

Michael breathes a sigh of relief. "Thanks Preston. I owe you one."

"Yeah, well don't thank me yet. Your wife can be very stubborn. Which runs in their family, you know.

Talking Alex into returning home is like hand-feeding a shark."

Michael musters up a smile after that remark. "That's my wife, alright."

"If the thought of your wife makes you smile like that, I better hurry up and get her home," Preston jokes. "Because man, you've been looking mighty withdrawn lately."

"That's because I've forgotten how to laugh or smile. These days I have nothing to be happy about."

"Hopefully this too shall pass, my man," Preston says, standing again. "Just like all the rest of the problems we encounter in life."

"I know you're trying to give me some encouragement, but this is not your everyday problem, Preston. This one is on a much larger scale," Michael says, getting up from his chair.

Walking over to escort Preston out, he is stopped in his tracks when Preston makes a statement. "By the way, you never mentioned why you're being blackmailed."

Before Michael can answer, Preston's cell phone rings. "Excuse me, man," he says, looking down at the caller ID. "I need to take this call."

"No problem," Michael answers, relieved he didn't have to answer.

Preston walks over to the other side of the room for privacy. "That was quick," he says into the phone in a low tone. "What you have for me?" He becomes silent as he listens.

Michael turns his back towards Preston to look out the window, wanting to ensure Preston that he respects his privacy. However does hear the ending to the call.

"Thanks man, I owe you," Preston says, then hangs up. "Sorry about that," he says as Michael turns to face him.

"No need to apologize," Michael responds with a wave of the hand. "I know you have other business to handle."

"Fortunately I do. If I didn't I wouldn't have a business." Putting his phone away he says, "I've got to run, man. If you need my help give me a jingle."

"You're helping me enough by talking to Alex. And that I will never forget." Michael goes over to shake Preston's hand. Preston slaps him on the back and leaves.

Michael walks over to the mirror and takes a good look at himself. Dark circles have developed under his eyes, and stubs from a new growth of beard are visible. His always neatly shaven head is forming an afro. "Damn, Preston was right," he says out loud. "I look haggard and depressed. Thank God I've been working from home, and for my buddy Melvin appearing for me in court. I've got to get a handle on this situation!"

Rubbing his unshaven face, he reaches for the phone. "Yes, this is Michael Crawford. I need to know when your next flight leaves for Washington D.C."

"Whisk right past me, why don't you."

"Oh baby, I'm sorry," Preston apologizes. He turns around to head towards the kitchen, where Ronnie is standing with her hands on her hips.

"And what do you have to say for yourself mister?" she teases.

"Guilty," he answers. He then grabs her around the waist and pulls her towards him. "I will never again walk into our home without acknowledging my woman," he promises, and gives her a kiss.

"What's the rush?" she asks after their lips parted. Instead of answering, Preston grabs her hand and leads her to the sofa. After sitting her down, he begins to explain. She looks at him, bewildered.

"I need to leave town right away, baby." When she tries to protest, he presses his hand against her mouth. "Now, no interruptions, okay, Ronnie?"

She nods.

"Baby," he says, sitting down beside her, "I must catch this flight in three hours. I also made a promise to Michael. And because I have to leave right away, it's impossible for me to do both. That's where you come in."

"Me?" she asks, surprised.

"Yes baby, you. I can't get into details, but I was supposed to go over to the hotel and convince Alex to return home."

"Why is Michael dragging you into their personal life?"

"I was already in it when Alex hired me to take those pictures, remember?"

"Okay, fine, go ahead and finish your story," she snaps.

Ignoring her attitude, he continues. "I want you to go in my place, to convince Alex to go home."

Ronnie becomes speechless. All she can do is stare at him in disbelief. Then suddenly she gets up off the sofa to walk away. Changing her mind, she stops. At that point Preston knows she will do it.

Slowly turning to face him, Ronnie starts speaking very calmly, with her arms folded across her chest.

"Preston, how do you expect me to convince Alex to go home? She has never listened to me. When we were growing up, Alex tried to boss everyone around. And she's still doing it."

Preston gets up and walks over to Ronnie, then unfolds her arms. Placing his hands on her shoulders he begins to explain. "Ronnie, it's important for you to talk to Alex. I really shouldn't be telling you this, but I have to so you'll understand why it's so important. But you can't tell Alex about this. Do you understand?"

She nods. Preston leads her back over to the sofa to sit down, then takes a deep breath and continues. "Michael is in real trouble. And I'm convinced more than ever that what Alex thinks is an affair, isn't. I can't tell you everything that's going on. But I can tell you this much. That woman Marlene is dealing with some dangerous people. Which means that both Michael and Alex could get hurt. That's why you need to try very hard to convince your sister to go home. She'd be safer there than at that hotel."

"Why is this woman trying to hurt both of my sisters?," Ronnie asks, tears falling down her cheeks.

"What do you mean baby?" he asks, wiping away the tears gently with his thumb.

"I was going to tell you about it last night," she says, "but you got in so late and I drifted off to sleep. Last night, Paris was so paranoid. She told us how two FBI agents showed up at her door. They wanted to talk to both Neil and her about that crazy woman Marlene. They've been watching her for a long time because she's been smuggling drugs, and they warned them to stay clear of her. Now Paris and Neil have to send the

boys to his mother to keep them out of harm's way."
Ronnie is crying now, barely getting the words out.

"Come here baby," he says, pulling her into his
arms, all the while thinking on ways to get Marlene out
of all their lives. Gently pulling away, he places his
hand under her chin to lift it up. "Look at me baby. I
love you, and I hate leaving you this way. But I have to
catch this flight. I'm going to pack a few things, and
you must pull yourself together. You can't let Alex see
how worried you are. She may become suspicious."

"I don't think I can pull it off," she says, sniffling.
"I may slip and tell her everything."

"You can handle it, you're my strong Nubian
Queen."

Ronnie smiles, unable to resist his charm. "Where
are you going, anyway?"

"Washington D.C.," he answers, getting up and
heading towards the bedroom.

Following him into the bedroom, Ronnie continues
to ask questions. "What's in Washington?"

"Answers, my love. I had a buddy run a check on
Marlene," he says, throwing clothes into the duffel
bag. "What I learned was very interesting. And it all
began in Washington."

"Preston, if those people are as dangerous as you
say they are, you can get hurt," she says with a worried
look.

"I'm going to be very careful."

"Is that all you're taking?"

"Yep, whatever else I need I'll buy when I get
there. But what I need right now is to taste those
luscious lips."

Ronnie throws her arms around his neck as if he isn't coming back. "Hold on here!" he responds to the display of affection. "I'll be back Ronnie. After all, we have a wedding to plan." He then kisses her long and hard.

Pulling away from their embrace, he grabs his duffel bag and throws it over his shoulders. He then winks and walks out of the bedroom.

Unable to watch him leave, for once Ronnie doesn't see him out. She listens as he gently shuts the door. Refusing to cry again, she walks into the bathroom to wash her face.

How am I going to talk Alex into going home? she ask herself after drying her face. Walking into the bedroom to change, Ronnie starts reflecting back on her life in Atlanta.

How simple it was then, and a lot less drama. As a matter of fact, it was very boring. Let's face it, I'm a city girl, and I like the hustle and bustle that goes on in a big city. And yes, a little drama is good for the soul. I only wish that I or my family wasn't involved in this one. Well, I guess it's time for me to go and give that Oscar-winning performance.

Grabbing her purse and keys, she hurriedly walks out the door. On her way to the car, she notices an attractive young man, around her son's age, walking towards the building. She says to herself, What I need to be doing is getting my nerves up and fly to San Antonio, to pay a visit to my handsome son and his family. When all of this is over, I'm taking that trip.

She gets into her Lexus and drives off. By the time she's on I96, her confidence begins to wane. Although she has to admit, using the wedding as an excuse to stop by is a good idea.

When it comes to organizing and party planning, she thinks, Alex is the one to go to. She loves taking control. But I'm no slouch in the organizational department either. That's where Alex and I are most alike.

With tears forming, Ronnie thinks about how organized their parents were. And how organizing that trip for seniors citizens brought about their death. All her parents had wanted to do was bring happiness into some old folks' lives. That trip to Florida was the last one they ever took. The bus driver had made sure of that by falling asleep at the wheel.

Ronnie shakes her head to clear away those unpleasant memories. Realizing she has reached the Renaissance Center, she pulls up to the Detroit Marriott Hotel for valet parking. Stepping out of her car, Ronnie pulls out a piece of paper with Alex's suite number on it.

Looking up from reading the number off the paper, Ronnie notices a couple walking past. They both look familiar to her, especially the woman. But she can't get a good look because the man is blocking her view.

I know I've seen her somewhere before, she says to herself. But where did I see her? Even the man looks a little familiar. And those features are so pronounced. I may not be sure of the man, but I'm sure about the woman.

As the man steps to the side, Ronnie gets a better look at the woman. "That's her!" Ronnie says, a little too loudly.

Covering her mouth with her hand, she starts walking with a fast pace towards the elevator. After reaching Alex's floor, she steps out of the elevator, looking around as if someone is following her. Comparing the number on the paper with the numbers on the wall, Ronnie starts heading in the direction which leads to Alex's suite.

Reaching the suite, Ronnie stands in front of the door to catch her breath. All of a sudden she feels a hand touch her shoulder. "Don't hurt me," she screams, dropping the magazines on the floor.

"What's wrong with you Ronnie?"

"Alex?" she asks slowly, turning around to make sure the voice matches the face.

"Yes, it's me and what in the world is going on!"

"A heart attack," Ronnie snaps. "Which you were on the verge of giving me. What possessed you to sneak up on me like that?"

"I wasn't sneaking," Alex snaps back. "So quit making a spectacle of yourself. The door is open, so pick up the magazines and get inside."

Before following Ronnie into the suite, Alex looks around to make sure no one witnessed that embarrassing scene. After shutting the door, Alex places her hands on her hips and stares at Ronnie in disbelief.

"What?" Ronnie asks.

"You know what," Alex answers. "You acted like a complete idiot out in that hallway," she says, pointing towards the door.

"No Alex, I acted like someone scared out of their wits. Anyway," she says, waving off Alex's comment. "I don't have to stay and listen to this."

"Okay, I'm sorry," Alex says, walking over to the sofa to sit next to Ronnie.

"You don't sound too sincere to me," Ronnie says, standing to leave. "I can get Paris to help with my wedding." She smiles to herself, knowing that will get to her.

Alex grabs her hand to stop her. "Please don't leave, Ronnie. I'm really sorry if I hurt your feelings by yelling at you. I was taking out my frustrations on you, and that wasn't fair. You're my sister, and I love you. I want to help make your wedding day special. What do you say?"

Looking down into Alex's hazel eyes, Ronnie knows her sister is sincere this time. "Okay, but next time I'm not going to forgive you so easily," she says, sitting back down.

Noticing the smirk on Ronnie's face, Alex starts smiling. All of a sudden they both break into laughter, then reach over to give each other a warm hug.

"Now, let's get started and plan a wedding," Alex says, squeezing Ronnie's hand.

"Fine with me sis," Ronnie responds, and pulls out her favorite magazine.

After an hour of looking at wedding dresses and discussing the colors, they decide to take a break.

"So what date did you two settle on?" Alex asks as she walks to the fridge to get them both a pop.

"June 17th."

"I've always wanted to be a June bride," Alex comments. "But in the end I guess it didn't matter, as long as I was a bride," she says, handing the pop to Ronnie. "I was even able to overlook his neurotic mother's behavior that day."

"You were the only one. I could have choked that old woman."

"I could have to, but I wasn't going to satisfy her by letting her spoil my big day. It really did turn out to be a wonderful day, didn't it Ronnie?"

"It sure did," Ronnie answers, listening to how Alex is reliving that day. Standing up, she walks over to her sister. "You miss Michael don't you?" Ronnie asks, placing her hand gently on Alex's shoulder.

"Yes I do, Ronnie, Alex says, turning around to face her. "And I'm tired of trying to remain strong, pretending I can handle it. When in reality I can't."

"Oh sis," Ronnie says, giving Alex a hug, at the same time thinking this is her opening.

After releasing their embrace, Ronnie steps back a little and places both hands on Alex shoulders. "I think maybe you should consider returning home. That's where you belong."

"I can't believe you're saying this to me Ronnie. Just because I opened up to you and showed my feelings, doesn't mean I've changed my mind. I want your support, not your advice."

"You need both," Ronnie says, thinking, The old Alex is back. "Besides, why should you inconvenience yourself, while Michael is living in the comfort of his home. It's your home too!" Work it girl, Ronnie says to herself. She continues, "Here you are holed up in this suite. As nice as it is Alex, it's still not home. All your beautiful expensive outfits and shoes are at home. Look at how you're dressed. You look like a ragamuffin."

"Don't you get it?" Alex exclaims. "I don't care about all those material things."

As Alex pops open her drink, Ronnie wonders what to say next. "Then what about the Glass Room?" she tries. "You love that room, and I know you have to miss it." Watching the look on Alex face when the Glass Room is mentioned gives Ronnie hope.

"I do love that room," Alex responds in a whisper. "I'm always at peace there. I could sit in there for hours on my chaise lounge, looking out at the lake," she says, visualizing herself in the room.

"Then go home," Ronnie says softly. "You don't belong here."

"How can I, with Michael there? I'll grow weak and eventually give in. Letting him off the hook is not what I want to do. He must be held accountable for what he did to me."

"I know you, sis, and you're not into the revenge thing."

"It's not about revenge, Ronnie. It's about getting my self respect back. I have to go to the bathroom."

As Alex leaves the room, Ronnie walks back over to the sofa to sit. What am I going to do now? she wonders. When that girl's on a mission, she's like a dog with a bone. I have to come out with the big guns, which means I have to break my promise to Preston. I'm sorry Preston, but my sister's safety is more important.

Alex's return disrupts Ronnie's train of thought. "Why don't we get back to planning your wedding," Alex insists. "I don't want to talk about Michael or going back home anymore."

Taking a deep breath, Ronnie decides to tell her what's going on. "Alex, I have something to tell you. I was sworn to secrecy not to release this information, but I guess I have to go back on my promise.

Alex, looking perplexed, stares into Ronnie's eyes, knowing what she is about to say is very important.

"Michael is not having an affair, Alex. At least that's what Preston feels. He doesn't know everything that's been going on, but he did manage to get some information out of Michael." Ronnie pauses for a moment, knowing she's about to break her promise.

"Don't stop now," Alex commands.

Taking another deep breath, Ronnie continues. "Anyway, what Preston found out was that Michael is being blackmailed by Marlene. And that she's being watched by the FBI for smuggling drugs. They're trying to capture this big-time drug lord she's been working for. And get this," Ronnie says, getting into the story. "She's the same woman who had an affair with Neil."

Alex perks up after hearing that. "You mean our brother-in-law Neil?"

"One in the same. You heard Paris last night. The FBI is following this woman. They've been staking out your house too, Alex."

"What you're telling me is very interesting, but it doesn't prove Michael isn't having an affair with that woman."

"It may not prove for certain he isn't having an affair, but it does leave room for doubt," Ronnie shoots back. "But the most important thing is that you could be in danger. These are very dangerous people. And you need to be in the safety of your own home, not leaving yourself open in this hotel."

"Come on Ronnie, don't be so dramatic. How in the world would these folks know where I am?"

"I'm sure they have their ways of finding things out. Besides, I saw that Marlene woman in the lobby with some man."

"So what?" Alex says, getting up and showing concern.

"What do you mean, so what," Ronnie spat. "For all you know, they could have followed you here. And if they don't know you're here, your paths will surely cross."

"I think you've been around Preston too long," Alex says snidely.

"Well it's a good thing I have. Because it leaves one less stupid person in this room!"

Alex swings around. "Don't you dare call me stupid!"

"Then quit acting like you are, and go into that bedroom and start packing. I'll help you. We don't know anything about the world that Marlene lives in. We're simple people. But I do know that her kind doesn't care about anything. You have to get past that pride of yours, and start thinking about your safety."

"How can I face Michael?" Alex asks, finally giving in.

Ronnie walks over to comfort her sister. With concern, she gently touches Alex's face. "I know how strong you are, Alex. Since you now know more about what's going on, you can open up a dialogue between you two."

"Thank you sis," Alex says, hugging Ronnie.

"Don't get mushy on me," Ronnie says, releasing her embrace. "That's not your style."

"Well, maybe it's time for a change. I think I'll start packing."

"That sounds like a good idea. I was thinking, Alex. Maybe you should call Michael to let him know you're coming home."

"Why should I do that? He'll see me when I get there."

"Because we may run into Marlene and that man. And if we don't show up, at least we would have alerted someone."

"There you go, thinking like Preston again. If I weren't sure before that you two belong together, I'm sure of it now. Okay, I'll call home."

Ronnie starts smiling as she watches Alex make the call.

"Are you sure of that, Doris?" Alex says into the phone. "Thanks, Doris." She hangs up the phone, then looks over at Ronnie. "Doris informed me that Michael went to Washington D.C.," she says with a puzzled look.

"That's strange," Ronnie responds. "Preston left for Washington today too. He mentioned that he had gotten some information about Marlene. So I'm assuming all the answers are in Washington."

"I'm going to Washington," Alex says suddenly as she rushes towards the bedroom.

"For what, Alex? What can you do?"

Alex spins around. "My husband is in some kind of trouble, and I need to be there with him."

"Whatever is going down, let them handle it, Alex! Preston is a professional. He knows what he's doing."

"Michael doesn't, Ronnie, he can get hurt." Looking confused, not knowing what to do next, Alex walks over to the phone.

"Now who are you calling?"

"The airlines. I'm booking the next flight to Washington D.C."

"I can't stop you, can I?" Ronnie asks.

"No you can't, so stop trying."

"Okay, fine, then make reservations for two. I'm going with you."

"I must be hearing things," Alex says, looking shocked. "You hate to fly."

"Well call me stupid, but I can't sit back and watch my sister walk into a dangerous situation alone. That is if I make it through the flight."

"You'll make it through," Alex says with a smile. "So why don't you go and throw a few things together. I'll call Les and Paris to let them in on what's going on."

"You know Paris will want to go with us, don't you."

"Yes, but she'd blow everything if she did."

"You're right. One look at Marlene would set her right off. I think our sister is an undercover hood rat."

"Get out of here and go pack, silly girl," Alex says smiling.

"Okay, I'm going. I'll see you at the airport. Oh, and Alex, please be careful."

"I will sis."

Ronnie grabs her purse and leaves.

Belinda Walker-Graham

CHAPTER ELEVEN

As Michael walks out of the airport doors, he notices his father signaling him from a black stretch limo. Michael is then met by the chauffeur, who retrieves his luggage and places them in the trunk of the limo. With the door open, Michael slides in next to his father, and greets him.

After the driver returns to the limo and seats himself behind the wheel, he turns to look back at Judge James Crawford.

"You can take us back to Palisades Park," the judge instructs.

"Yes sir," the chauffeur responds, and drives off.

"Thanks for picking me up," Michael comments.

"If I had agreed to go with your mother to Martha's Vineyard, you would have been on your own. So what's the urgency, son? I thought the meeting was supposed to be in Detroit."

"It was. But I decided to take it out of Detroit and meet in Washington instead."

"Why would you do that?" his father asks, slightly agitated. "It's too close to home, Michael. You can cause a lot of suspicion meeting with those shady people. We're too well known here."

"I'm willing to take that chance," Michael says, staring out the window. "Mother has finally rubbed off on you, hasn't she Dad?"

"And what is that suppose to mean?"

"It means that all you think about is yourself. Did you ever consider what this would do to my marriage, or Alex? She didn't have anything to do with this, but she's right smack in the middle now. I won't allow her to be brought into this mess."

"So that's why you brought the meeting here?"

"Yes Dad, it is, and it's too late to change it."

"I hope you know what you're doing, Michael. If you don't, the consequence can be dire. Both of our careers will be in jeopardy. Even your mother will catch heat from all of this."

Michael turns towards his father with a surprised look on his face. "When did you start caring about anyone but yourself? You have everyone fooled. But remember, I know the truth."

Staring back at his son, James only makes one comment. "I sure hope you've given this new strategy some serious thought." He then turns away.

Choosing not to comment, Michael looks on as the driver pulls onto US 50, heading towards their destination.

"Hey Pres, over here man," Zack yells. "And hurry up before I have to move!"

Preston starts walking at a faster pace. "I can't believe you're on time, Zack. This has got to be a first."

"Go to hell man, and get in," Zack chuckles.

Preston throws his bags in the back of the Cadillac SUV and hops in. "Want to stop for a drink before heading to the Best Western?" Zack asks.

"Not on this trip," Preston answers. "This case is involving family, and I need all my wits about me to stay on top of the game. I don't want to waste one minute being unproductive." Zack nods in understanding. "Also," Preston continues, "I've changed hotels. I'll be staying at the Lombardy instead."

"The whole purpose of my booking the Best Western was for you to be near the FBI building."

"I don't need to be near the FBI building. I have, you my man," Preston says, slapping Zack on the back. "So what else do you have for me?"

"Per your request, I put a tail on Michael right after we hung up. He's here, Pres. Arrived about 30 minutes before you. I saw him get into a limo."

"Well I'll be damned. This is getting more and more interesting. Are you sure it was him? After all, you've only seen a picture of him once."

"Pres, you should know not to doubt me. I have a photographic memory. I'm also certain it was his old man waving to him from the limo."

"I have a gut feeling this is not a family visit," Preston says. "Michael desperately wants to bring this whole blackmailing business to an end. The fear of Alex getting hurt has prompted him into action instead of moping around."

"So maybe he's setting up a meeting here to draw attention away from Alex."

"Good assumption," Preston agrees. "But there's more."

Before leaving, Zack looks over at Preston, curious, then slowly pulls off. After turning onto Pennsylvania Avenue, Zack decides to break Preston's concentration. "You're too quiet, man. What's going on in that mind of yours?"

"I'm sorry, man. You know how I get when I'm involved with a case. But I was thinking about what you told me back at the airport."

"What was that?"

"When you told me about Michael's old man in the limo." Noticing how Zack looks puzzled, Preston continues. "Michael has a very good income, but his folks got the real bucks. I'm beginning to wonder if dear old dad is involved somehow."

"Or at the very least financing the payoff. Well Pres, here's our stop, 2019 Pennsylvania Ave."

"Okay man, thanks for the ride. I need you to do a check on Judge Crawford. I'm sure you'll find something that's been sealed off from the public."

"You got it, man. Helping you solve your case will help me get Shark. I want him off the face of the earth for putting that poison in my sister's veins. She knew too much, and he made sure she didn't talk," he says with sadness in his voice.

"I know man," Preston agrees. "I loved Capri too. She was like a sister to me. We'll get the bastard this time."

"We better, Pres. This may be our last chance. Those punk asses Farley and Moss have been screwing up since they got the case."

"We have to make sure we get to Shark before they do. And we're one step ahead. I'm going to check in now, you go home and get some rest. We have a lot of work ahead of us."

"Okay man, talk to you tomorrow."

Preston watches Zack pull off, then goes into the hotel to check in. After checking his room out, he decides to take a walk.

As he strolls down Pennsylvania Ave, he passes a couple holding hands. At that moment he longs for

Ronnie to be by his side, wishing she was there in Washington, instead of Detroit.

"I will never get on a plane with you again!"

"What did I do Alex?" Ronnie asks, dragging her luggage while trying to keep up. When Alex stops in an attempt to answer, Ronnie runs right into her and hits the back of her heel. "Oh, I'm so sorry Alex," she apologizes, letting go of her luggage to assist her sister.

"Go away Ronnie!" Alex screams. Ronnie steps back in amazement as Alex continues to berate her. "You've been a pain from the second we boarded that plane. You screamed when we took off. And during the whole flight you bothered the attendants, asking if the plane was going down every time we felt turbulence! And now this!" she yells, pointing at her heel.

"Are you through scolding me?" Ronnie asks calmly. "Because if you are, I would like to leave Washington International Airport and get to our hotel to freshen up. That is, if you don't mind."

Without saying a word, Alex picks up her luggage and hobbles off in a huff. Knowing her calmness ticked Alex off even more, Ronnie smiles and follows.

Once outside, Alex spots an empty cab. "Come on Ronnie, lets grab that cab before someone else does."

Just as Alex is about to head towards the cab, Ronnie reaches over to retrieve the luggage out of her hands. "I'll carry that," she says, smiling at her sister.

Shocked at the gesture, Alex slowly releases the handle. She smiles back at Ronnie to let her know all is forgiven. They both head towards the cab, one hobbling, the other struggling with two sets of luggage.

When the cab driver sees how Ronnie is struggling, he immediately rushes over to retrieve the luggage. "Where are you beautiful ladies headed?" he asks.

"Four Seasons Hotel," Alex answers as she and Ronnie slide into the cab.

After placing the luggage into the trunk, the driver gets into the cab. "Did you say Four Seasons Hotel?" he repeats.

"Yes, so can we get going now," Alex snaps. "We're very tired."

"Whatever your heart desires, beautiful lady," he responds, and takes off.

"Look at him driving like a bat out of hell," Ronnie whispers to Alex. "Why did you encourage him?"

"I didn't tell him to drive like we're on a speedway," she whispers back. "I merely informed him that we were tired, and wanted to get going."

"I feel like I'm back in that plane," Ronnie mumbles.

"That just goes to show, you're no safer on the ground," Alex comments. Ronnie stares at her for a second, then turns away to look at the scenery. Alex leans her head back with a smile of satisfaction on her face.

A sudden stop brings them out of their individual trances. "Four Seasons Hotel," the cabby informs them. "You see, I got you here very fast. Just as you asked, beautiful lady."

"Whatever," Alex responds, opening the door for them to get out.

After setting their luggage out and receiving his fee, the driver gets into his cab and takes off, burning rubber. "I guess he's off to pick up the next passenger to scare the hell out of," Ronnie comments.

"Well, all I can say is that, I pity the fool," Alex responds, trying to sound like Mr. T.

"Oh no you don't," Ronnie laughs. "Not Miss Prissy trying to have some humor. And of all people to imitate. I like you better being prissy."

"Don't worry, I'll return to my old self when this mess is all over. I guess I'm trying to make light of a bad situation."

"Maybe we should hit a comedy club or two while we're here," Ronnie suggests while grabbing her luggage.

"For what?" Alex asks, looking puzzled.

"If you insist on making light of a bad situation by trying to be humorous, then what better place for you to go than to a comedy club? Maybe you can pick up some tips, which would make my short stay here bearable."

"This is not a pleasure trip Ronnie," Alex says as they walk towards the entrance of the hotel.

"Maybe not, but we need something to take our minds off whatever we're getting ready to encounter."

"We'll see. All I want is a good night's rest. I'm tired of thinking."

Ronnie nods in agreement as they walk into the hotel.

"Good morning, son. Have you had breakfast yet?"

"No, Dad. How can I eat when our careers are at stake?"

"You worry too much, son," Judge Crawford says, lighting a cigar.

"If I recall, you were the one up in arms last night. What brings about this change?"

"Well Michael, I was doing a lot of thinking last night. We really have the upper hand. Money and power, which is a wonderful combination, will give us the control. They want what we have very badly. And because of that, it's time to negotiate. We can bring an end to this mess once and for all."

"Okay Dad," Michael says, walking onto the lanai. "But what makes you think those slimes will keep their word? They may agree with whatever we come up with. But greed will rear its ugly head, and they'll want more."

"Sit down son. We'll continue this in one second. Hilda!" he calls out. "Whip my son and I up some breakfast please. Now where were we? Oh yes, you mentioned greed. Michael, all I can say is that it's time to end this. And I firmly believe we can negotiate and come up with a figure to make everyone happy. So I want you to call that tramp, and set up a meeting with her and that slime ball she works for."

"Whatever you say, Dad. I want to get this over with quickly so I can work on getting my marriage back on track with Alex. So let's get down to business. Tell me what you want me to do."

"Now Michael, we need to get this done tonight. Your mother is coming home in a couple of days. The meeting must be at an out of the way place where no one can recognize you, understood?"

"Yes Dad, but where do you suggest? Oh I forgot, you're used to frequenting out of the way places."

"Don't get flip with me Michael. Now, it's this place called Track 2000. It's a club near the Navy

Yard. Some of everybody goes there, from drag queens to lesbians."

"Why Track 2000, Dad? Mirage is near the Navy Yard and out of the way."

"You'd be less conspicuous at Track 2000, Michael. Please don't question me, and do as I say. I've made it this far by sheer determination and intelligence. I overcame every obstacle that got in my way. That's why I'm a success."

Looking into his son's face from across the table brings on a surge of emotion. Judge Crawford stops for a second, then continues. "And I have to admit, son, being a little shrewd helped," he adds, waiting on Michael's reaction.

Not believing what he heard, Michael leans forward. "Shrewd!" he says, surprised. "I know you're not perfect. I've witnessed too much lately to know better. But shrewd? I thought that was more mother's department."

With a smirk, James shakes his head before responding. "This is a dog eat dog world, son. Sometimes you have to take what's due to you. As the old cliché' goes, 'Nice guys always finish last.' And I had every intention of succeeding, which I did. Besides, you definitely benefited from it."

"Boy were my eyes closed," Michael says, leaning back again. I guess I really don't know you at all, do I Dad?"

Before his father can answer, Hilda enters with their breakfast. "Thank you Hilda," he says with a smile. "That will be all." Hilda nods, smiles at Michael, then leaves.

"Michael you must trust me on this, he continues, digging into his eggs. "When that tramp calls you, insist on meeting at our designated place. If she refuses, call her bluff. I can guarantee, they'll start singing a different tune."

"It's your call, Dad. But if it doesn't go down right, I'm distancing myself from this whole mess."

"Eat up, my boy," he commands, not giving any credence to Michael's comment. "You can't think on an empty stomach."

As Michael begins to eat, his cell phone rings. He looks up at his father, then answers.

It's Marlene. "Ready for the big day?" she asks.

"I'm ready to get you out of our lives," he responds.

"You may very well get your wish, sugar," she says. "That is, if the price is right. So listen up while I give you the instructions."

"I think not, Marlene. I want you to listen up, because you're no longer calling the shots."

"Oh is that right?"

"Yes that's right," he answers with authority. "We're going to do things my way, or the whole deal is off."

"You don't want to do that, Michael," she says in a harsh tone. "The media will have a field day with your family. Not to mention your careers."

"Go ahead Marlene. Give it your best shot. But trust me when I say, we will have the upper hand. We'll take the heat for a while. But it will die down eventually. You see, I come from a strong family, and a powerful one. We know the law, and will use it to our advantage. I suggest you play by our rules or not play at all."

"Well, well, Michael, you're full of surprises! I wonder if it's because dear old dad is calling the shots. Because we both know you don't have the guts."

"Doesn't take guts to deal with gutter rats," he snaps. "Now are we still on for tonight, or not?"

"Oh we're on, sugar. Name the place and time for us to meet, and we'll be there."

"What do you mean we?" he asks, surprised.

"Did I forget to tell you about my boss?" she answers snidely. "He's coming too, Michael. I'm sure the old man will be there."

"No he won't," Michael snaps.

"What a pity," she says, pretending to be sad. "I was so hoping to see him. I guess it will be the three of us, right Michael? Because if you've involved anyone else, there will be hell to pay. Starting with your beautiful wife."

Stunned from what he heard, Michael becomes quiet. "I can't hear you Michael!" Marlene sings.

He finally speaks up. "No one else is involved."

"If that's the case, you have nothing to worry about. My time is precious, so let's get the ball rolling."

"What you got for me, Zack?" Preston asks while getting into the SUV.

"Man, wait until you hear this. Our buddy Spike came through for us, man. He was able to bug the livable parts of the house."

"How's that coming through, Zack? It was a job half done."

"Come on Mr. Perfectionist," he jokes. "He did what he could on short notice."

"I guess I have to be satisfied with that," Preston responds, looking disappointed.

"That's not all," Zack says. "There's something else you should know." Preston looks over at Zack curious. "On my way over here, I saw Ronnie and one fine sister coming out of the Four Seasons Hotel."

"You what!" Preston yells, taken totally off guard. "Are you sure?"

"Yeah man. You know I like looking at fine sisters. And when I saw those two coming out of the hotel, I did a double take. I recognized Ronnie, but not the other sister."

"That had to be Alex," Preston remarks. Zack looks at him with interest. "Down boy," Preston commands. "She hasn't left Michael yet. Did you see where they were headed?"

"Sure did, Pres. From what I could tell looking through my rearview mirror, they were headed towards the Café."

"That's just great," Preston says, visibly angry. "Now I have to try and keep Ronnie and Alex out of this mess!"

"You take care of your woman," Zack instructs. "I'll look out for Alex."

"Look is all you'll get a chance to do, my brother. Now start this big escalade up. We're going to surprise a couple of ladies I know."

"You got it," Zack responds happily.

"I'm so glad we came here to eat," Ronnie comments. "These selections on this menu looks great."

"I knew you'd like it," Alex responds. "I only suggest the best."

"Go ahead girl and give yourself a pat on the back, as usual."

Alex starts patting her own back with a chuckle. "You know Alex," Ronnie says, looking serious. "Preston will kill me if he knows I'm here."

"Why are you looking so worried? We won't run into Preston. Besides, we're out of here in the morning. You'll probably beat Preston back home anyway." Changing the subject, Alex continues talking, not giving Ronnie a chance to reply. "I'm going over to see Michael this evening to try and get some answers."

"What if you don't get the answers you're looking for?"

"I'll cross that bridge when I get there."

"Well answer this, Alex. What am I supposed to be doing while you're pumping Michael for information? Because I'm not staying held up in that hotel."

"Then go to that comedy club you mentioned yesterday."

"I don't want to go alone, Alex. That's no fun."

"Ronnie, I'm sure you can find something to do."

"Okay fine," Ronnie gives in. "I'm a resourceful kind of girl, I'll find something."

"Let's order, I'm starved," Alex says insistently. Looking over the menu again, she decides what she wanted to order. As she looks up from the menu to flag the waiter, she freezes.

219

Not knowing what Alex is staring at so intensely, Ronnie turns towards the direction of Alex's eyes, to see Preston and Zack approaching their table. She turns to Alex and says, "I'm dead."

"What are you talking about? He has too much sense to kill you in front of all of these folks," Alex laughs.

"You're no help, Alex," she whispers.

"Oh Ronnie, what's the big deal? All you have to do is charm your way out of this."

"How close are they now?"

"Look behind you."

Ronnie slowly turns and looks up into Preston face. "Hey baby," she says, smiling.

"Now I know why I couldn't reach you last night," he responds, not smiling back. "Scoot your butt over," he instructs in a low tone, then eases into the booth next to her. Zack sits next to Alex.

"Hello Alex," Preston says.

"Hi Preston," she answers, smiling. She turns to Zack and extends her hand. "My name is Alex, and yours?"

"Zack," he says, accepting her hand with a big grin. "Hey Ronnie, what's up?"

"I'm waiting to find out," she comments. Zack holds his head down and chuckles.

"Now that the formalities are over, what the hell are you two doing here?" Preston asks, looking at Ronnie.

"It's all my fault," Alex pipes in. "I found out Michael was in Washington, and I wanted to know why. So I decided to fly here, and Ronnie didn't want me to go alone."

"Is that so?" he questions. "And how did you know Michael was in Washington?"

"My God Preston, you're full of questions," Alex says.

"That's because there's more to this story than you're letting on."

"Okay Preston," Ronnie says, deciding to come clean. "I told Alex about Michael being blackmailed, and the danger surrounding her, to get her to go home. When she found out by Doris that Michael was here, she decided to fly to Washington to get some answers. She needed my support, so I accompanied her."

"It wasn't a good idea for you two to come here," Preston says, frustrated.

"My marriage is at stake, Preston," Alex says. "I need answers that only Michael can provide."

"I sympathize with your dilemma, Alex. However, this involves more than just your marriage. Your very lives may be at stake too. These are very dangerous people we're dealing with. And you two are putting yourselves right in the middle. Zack and I are running against the clock. It's going to be hard for us to concentrate on this case and watch the both of you at the same time."

"I'm sorry, Preston," Ronnie says, apologetic. "I didn't mean to cause any distractions."

"I know you didn't, but that's exactly what you're doing."

"Stop it Preston," Alex insists. "You're really scaring me. It can't be that serious."

"It is that serious," Zack interrupts. "Pres is only trying to protect the both of you."

221

Preston takes a deep breath before continuing. "We need the both of you to make a promise to us."

"What's that, baby?" Ronnie asks.

"We're going to take the two of you back to the hotel. We want you to stay in your room until you hear from us."

Ronnie is quick to agree. Alex is hesitant, but finally agrees to get Preston off their backs.

Just as Preston is about to continue talking, the waiter approaches. "I apologize for the delay, but we're very busy. I also wanted to give the gentlemen time to decide on what to order, since they joined you late."

"I'm not hungry anymore," Ronnie says.

"Neither am I," Alex joins in.

"I'd like a cup of coffee," Preston says. "What about you Zack?"

"Yeah, coffee for me too."

The waiter leaves and shortly returns with their coffee. After he leaves, Preston continues where he left off.

"Since we have your word not to leave the room, I'm going to explain something to you." Anxious to hear, Ronnie and Alex give Preston their full attention. "The reason it's so important for you two to keep your word, is because we're expecting something to go down sometime tonight. Zack and I are hooking up with an informant this evening. We're hoping to get all the information needed to bring this case to an end."

"And we're not sure where this will lead us," Zack interrupts. "Now do you understand why it's important for you beautiful ladies to lay low?"

Ronnie and Alex, remaining silent, nod their heads in response. With nothing else left to say, Preston signals the waiter for the bill. After paying, Preston stands up to leave. "Ready everyone?" he asks.

"Let's ride," Zack responds, sliding out of the booth, followed by Ronnie and Alex.

All four leave the Café. Not a word is spoken on the short ride back to the hotel. Ronnie sits snuggled up to Preston in the back seat, worried about what might happen. Zack is humming *Happy Feelings* by Frankie Beverly. He's thrilled to have Alex sitting up front with him, and wishing the ride was longer.

"Okay ladies, this is your stop," Zack announces.

"Thank you Zack," Alex says, expressing her gratitude.

"You're welcome, pretty lady," Zack replies. Alex then opens the door and steps out of the vehicle. "By the way, I love your Cadillac SUV," she says.

"Why thank you, Alex," Zack responds with a grin.

Alex smiles back at him, shuts the door, and moves away from the vehicle. What a hunk, she says to herself. He's working those jeans with that nice tight butt. If I wasn't married I'd definitely give him a taste of me.

Looking back at Zack, she notices he's staring at her. Feeling embarrassed about her thoughts, she turns her back to the SUV.

"Did you see Alex flirting with Zack?" Ronnie asks.

"That's good," Preston responds. "She needs a little distraction right now. It's all good, baby. Now back to you. I mean it when I said this is a dangerous situation. I hope you keep your promise to stay put

223

tonight. I can't afford to go to prison for killing the person who harms you. A cop is dead meat in there."

"We won't leave the hotel until we hear from you."

"That's my girl," he says, kissing her forehead. "We have to go now, baby."

"Promise me you'll take care of yourself," she insists, looking into his eyes.

"Don't I always come back to you?"

She nods. Preston gives her a passionate kiss, then eases her out of the vehicle.

After he gets up front with Zack, Preston looks out at Ronnie with such longing that it draws her back to the vehicle. He opens the window. "I love you," she says.

"I love you too, baby." He then turned to Zack. "It's that time, man."

Ronnie steps back as Zack pulls off. Before she turns to join Alex, she notices a piece of paper by the curb. "Preston must have dropped this when he stepped out of the vehicle," she says. She opens up the folded paper and reads what's written on it. "What's Track 2000?"

"What did you say?" Alex asks.

"I was just talking to myself," she answers, putting the paper in her jeans pocket.

"Well, I'm ready to go inside so I can change."

"For what? We're not going anywhere."

"You may not be, but I am," Alex remarks as they enter the hotel. "I'm still going to see Michael, no matter what Preston said."

"You're going to ignore Preston's warning?" Ronnie asks, hitting the elevator button.

"That's your man, not mine," Alex snaps. "He can't tell me what to do."

On the ride up to their floor, both women are very quiet. Once inside their room, Alex immediately heads towards the bathroom to shower. Ronnie paces the room trying to figure out what to do. If I could, she says to herself, I'd lock her in the bathroom,. Maybe Les would know what to do. That's it! I'll call Les.

Ronnie walks over to the phone and punches in Les's number.

"Hello," the voice on the other end answers.

"Paris, what are you doing answering Les's phone?"

"And hello to you too," Paris replies, ignoring the question.

"I'm sorry, but I have a situation here and I need advice from Les," Ronnie says.

"Alex is acting up, isn't she?" Paris asks.

"As usual. She never listens to anyone."

"Better you than me having to deal with her. If anyone can handle her, it's you, Ronnie."

"Where's Les?"

"This is going to shock you, so sit down. Les is upstairs as we speak, getting ready for a date."

"A date!" Ronnie is astonished. "She and Steve have been separated only about a minute!"

"I know, but Steve made it clear to her that the marriage is over, and he's moving to San Francisco. So why should Les waste any time starting her new life?"

"You do have a point. Who is this guy, anyway?"

"I've never met him. All I know is that he was referred to her to do the renovating on her shop. They hit it off right away, and he asked her out. From what

225

she tells me, he's really nice, and has his own business. Look Ronnie, Les is very nervous about this date, so now is not the time to lay all this about Alex on her."

"You're right. If she ask about the call, tell her I was checking on you guys."

"Sure will," Paris says. "And Ronnie, be careful. I've been worried every since you two left for Washington. Alex should have waited until Michael returned. But knowing Preston is there makes me feel a little better. Oh, and good luck with handling Alex."

"Thank you sis, I need it."

"I love you guys," Paris says.

"I know," Ronnie replies softly. "We love you too."

After hanging up, Ronnie can hear Alex moving around. She's actually going through with this, Ronnie says to herself.

Suddenly Alex steps out of the bedroom, twirling around in a purple silk, low cut dress. "So what do you think?" she asks.

"You look great Alex," Ronnie answers. "You're showing quite a bit of cleavage, girl. Is this your secret weapon to get Michael to talk?"

"No it's not," Alex snaps. "I only want him to see what he's throwing away."

"Why can't you wait until we hear from Preston?" Ronnie pleads. "It's not safe for you to go to Michael right now."

"I'm only going to his parent's home, which is very safe. Their home is gated, and it has the best security system money can buy."

Ronnie throws her hands up. "I give up," she says, exasperated. "Please watch your back, okay?"

"I will sis," Alex says lovingly. She walks over to Ronnie and gives a sisterly hug. "It will be okay, I promise." Grabbing her purse, she looks over at Ronnie and points her finger at her. "Make sure you're here when I get back. I might need a shoulder." With that she smiles at her sister and leaves.

Oh God, what am I to do now? Ronnie asks herself, looking up at the ceiling. I don't have a good feeling about this.

All of a sudden, an idea pops into her head. She reaches into her jeans pocket and pulls out the piece of paper she found. Looking at it, she realizes this must be the place Preston and Zack are meeting their informant. She reaches for the hotel key and runs out the door.

"He hasn't shown up yet," Zack comments.

"Don't worry, man," Preston assures him. "He'll show, trust me. According to the tape, the meeting is to take place around 8 p.m. We have 15 minutes to go." He looks down at his watch, then looks up in time to spot Michael standing in front of the building. "Bingo! I knew he'd show."

"Let's go," Zack says, sounding anxious.

"Hold on, Zack. He's only standing around right now waiting."

"He looks as if he's ready to shit his pants," Zack says, observing Michael.

"You would too if you're not used to this kind of scene. This is a culture shock for him. We'll wait right here until the scum shows up. Then we'll make our move."

Preston and Zack wait 45 minutes before deciding to act. "I think it's time to mingle," Preston says. "Michael's beginning to get impatient, and starting to walk around. We can't afford to lose him."

Just as they're opening the SUV door, Preston spots what looks to be a woman heading towards Michael. "Do you see what I see Zack?"

"I'm on it man," Zack answers.

"Let's go then!" Preston yells, jumping out of the SUV.

They start moving at a fast pace. The closer they get, the clearer the view of the woman becomes. With people standing in front of her it's difficult to identify her, but as the people start moving around they get a better look.

"That's Ronnie!" Preston shouts. He and Zack both start running towards Michael and Ronnie, who begin to walk away.

"They're leaving, Pres!" Zack shouts as they push people out of their way. But the closer they get, the further away Michael and Ronnie become. "Oh shit Pres!," Zack gasps, "they're headed towards the parking lot. What now?" He stops running and tries to catch his breath.

"Well, it's too late to stop them now," Preston answers, frustrated. "I would have called out to her, if I thought for a second she could hear me."

"With this crowd Pres, there's no way your voice would have carried. Come on man," Zack says, patting Preston on the back. Both men turn and head back to their vehicle.

"Why do you think Ronnie showed up here?" Zack asks. "We didn't tell her where we were going. How could she have known?"

Preston, staring into space, doesn't answer. Upon reaching the SUV, he suddenly has a revelation. "That's it!" he shouts.

"What?"

"Those scums didn't show, because they're at Michael's parents'. The club was only a diversion."

"How did you come to that conclusion?"

"Think about it, man. Michael's old man has been involved all along. At first, ignoring my gut instinct, I felt he was trying to protect his son. But he's too close to the situation. And remember on the tape, Marlene thought the old man was going to show, because we heard Michael tell her the old man wasn't coming."

"If you're right, Pres, Michael and Ronnie may be walking into a bad situation if that's where they're headed."

Preston looks over at Zack, then jumps into the vehicle. Zack follows suit, and once inside he takes off, burning rubber. "I'm still confused, Pres," he says. "How did Ronnie know where to go?"

"From me," Preston answers. "I was looking for the address I wrote down on a piece of paper. The name of the club was written on that paper too. When I reached into my pocket, it wasn't there. I believe it fell out when we dropped them off at the hotel. Ronnie must have picked it up and put everything together. I have a smart woman, you know."

"But why would she come there?"

229

"I can bet that Alex didn't listen to us, and left to go see Michael. Ronnie went there to find us, but ran into Michael instead.

"It's time to find out what else Spike dug up for us," Preston continues, reaching for his cell. "We have more players in the game, and one happens to be Ronnie. I will not let anything happen to her."

"I feel you, man," Zack says as he ran his second red light.

"Michael, slow down!"

"You don't understand, Ronnie. We need to get to my parents as soon as possible."

"What's the hurry!" she screams.

"When you asked me why I was at that club, I didn't answer you. I was there to meet the woman who's blackmailing me, and that bum she's working for, but they didn't show."

As Michael talks, Ronnie thinks about what Preston had told them at the Café. It wasn't an informant they were meeting, she thinks to herself. They were casing the place.

"Are you listening to me, Ronnie?"

"Yes Michael, I am. But you still didn't explain the need to rush to your parents. Alex isn't going anywhere until she talks to you."

"That's my point! I don't want her there. It may not be safe. Since they didn't show up at that club, no telling where they are, or what they may do."

"Your parents' home is like Fort Knox. At least that's what Alex told me."

"Maybe so, Ronnie. But where there's a will there's a way, if someone wants to get you."

Since Ronnie can't convince Michael to slow down, she becomes quiet and prays this wouldn't be her last ride. As they enter the gates, Ronnie breathes a sigh of relief. She becomes relaxed and takes in the beautiful view. There's a fountain in the middle of the circular drive. And even though it's dark, she notices how beautiful the landscape is. But nothing can compare to the magnificent mansion they're approaching.

"Oh Michael, this is breathtaking."

"Thank you Ronnie. This is my home away from home. And the only thing my mother truly loves."

Ronnie looks over at Michael with sympathy as he brings the Jag to a halt. He jumps out of the car and rushes towards the house. Ronnie follows, barely able to keep up.

Once inside, Michael starts calling out Alex's name. But the only voice he hears is that of his mother's. She's standing at the entrance of the study.

"Mother, what are you doing here?" Michael asks, surprised to see her.

"Hello son," she says, arms stretched out. "Come give your mother a hug."

Michael approaches his mother, wondering what brought on this change, and gently embraces her.

"Hello Mrs. Crawford," Ronnie says, stepping forward.

"Hello my dear. It's nice seeing you again."

Getting impatient, Michael interrupts. "Mother, where's Alex?"

Changing her expression, Beatrice turns and faces the study. Michael walks pass his mother, followed by

Ronnie. They enter the study. Michael's father and Alex are sitting like mannequins, looking bewildered.

"Alex," Michael calls out softly.

"Hi Michael," she answers, in a subdued tone.

Sensing something is wrong, Michael looks over at his father. "What's going on Dad?"

"I can answer that for you, sugar," says a voice behind him.

Michael whips around to find Marlene walking towards him from the direction of the sliding door. She's holding a gun.

"What in the hell are you doing here in my parents home?" Michael snarls.

"We decided to pay a visit to dear old dad," Marlene answers, "since he refused to meet with us."

"What do you mean, we," Michael asks.

"Nice of you to join us Michael," a husky voice behind them says.

Michael and Ronnie both turn around to see where the voice is coming from. In walks a physically fit, attractive bald headed man. Beatrice is walking ahead of him, with his gun pointed at her back.

Pushing Beatrice towards where James and Alex are sitting, the man stares over at Ronnie. "I see you brought another guest, Michael. And such a beautiful one at that. Now go over and sit with the rest," he instructs her.

Ronnie eases over and sits next to Alex on the mauve leather sofa, then throws her arms around Alex.

"I should have listened to Preston," Alex says nervously. "I'm really scared, Ronnie."

Releasing her embrace, Ronnie rubs Alex face. "It's going to be okay, Alex. I'm sure Preston is looking for us," she whispers.

"I hope he finds us in time," Alex says.

"Hey, quit the whispering!" Marlene yells. "And aren't you the bitch who got in my face at the restaurant?"

"I don't know what you're talking about," Ronnie answers.

"Oh yes you do! You're Paris's sister." Walking over to Ronnie, Marlene whispers in her ear. "Neil sure was a good fuck," she says, and starts laughing.

"Step back, Marlene!" Shark shouts.

Stepping back, Marlene continues. "And tell that bitch sister of yours that she's dead meat," she says coldly.

Ronnie immediately turns to Alex. "Why didn't you speak up and say you were Paris's sister too?"

"Why should I? I have enough problems being Michael's wife."

"You two are being very bad," Shark comments. "When I say no whispering, that's exactly what I mean. The both of you may be beautiful, but I won't hesitate to kill you. Michael, I suggest you join your family over there," he says, waving the gun in their direction.

Michael does as he's told and sits on the floor by Alex. He then looks up at her, apologizing with his eyes. She reaches down and gently takes his hand, letting him know everything is okay.

A clap of the hand by Shark draws them out of their trance. "We don't want to be rude to our guest," he says, "but we have to leave shortly. But before we do, there's some business we must take care of."

Everyone starts staring at each other, not knowing what's going to happen next. "Old man," Shark says, looking over at James. "I think you owe us something."

"He doesn't owe you anything!" Beatrice spits.

"Calm down, Beatrice," James insists, patting her thigh. "This won't get us anywhere."

"I think you better listen, old lady," Shark suggests. "Because if you don't, your husband will be living the rest of his life without a mate. Okay old man, get up!"

James weakly stands up. "Now," says Shark, "I want you to take me to where you stashed the money."

"No, James," Beatrice begs, grabbing his arm. "I forgive you, and I'm sorry for what I put you through."

"I know, honey," he whispers. "I have regrets as well. I wish you hadn't cut your vacation short, Beatrice. Bringing you into this mess I created is tearing me apart."

Beatrice stares at him with curious eyes. "Get going old man!" Shark yells. As James starts to move, Beatrice's grip loosens.

"Hold it right there!" Zack shouts as he enters from the side of the lanai.

Marlene immediately freezes and drops her gun. Shark heads towards the entrance of the study, then suddenly stops. As he backs up into the study, a figure comes into view. It's Preston, walking him back into the study with a gun pointing at his chest. "Drop your gun, Shark," Preston demands.

Shark slowly eases his grip on the gun until it falls to the floor.

"Now go and join your partner," Preston says. Zack pushes Marlene towards Shark while Preston picks up the gun.

"You two low-lives are never going to see the light of day again," Zack says.

Shark looks over at Zack and smiles. "I'm sorry I didn't attend Capri's funeral," he says.

Zack, visibly shaken, raises his gun towards Shark.

"You don't want to do that, Zack," Preston insists. "It's not worth it, man. And it won't bring your sister back."

"But it will feel damn good, Pres, to blow his head off." Zack looks over at Preston, then lowers his gun.

"Are you all okay?" Preston asks the others. They answer "Yes" in unison. Preston looks over at Ronnie and winks. When she smiles at him, Shark takes notice.

Michael stands up and pulls Alex on her feet to join him. "Are you okay sweetheart?"

"I'm a little shaken, but I'll be fine," she says. He pulls her close and gives her a big hug. James puts his arms around Beatrice and kisses her on the forehead.

"The cops should be here soon," Zack announces.

"It's all your fault!" Marlene screams suddenly at Beatrice.

"Are you directing your venom at me?" Beatrice asks.

"Look at you!" Marlene snarls. "Still a cold hearted bitch!"

"Do I know you, young lady?" Beatrice asks calmly.

"Oh, you don't remember me, do you? Well let me refresh your memory. You're responsible for sending me to prison. I told you I didn't know about the armed robbery. My ex was the only one involved."

"If you were sentenced to serve time," Beatrice says, "it's only because the jury found you guilty. I had to sentence you according to the law."

"And that's why I fucked your husband. And he loved every minute of it. As a matter of fact, he told me he couldn't stand your crusted old pussy!"

"James, is that true?" Beatrice asks, looking hurt.

"No honey, it isn't. We were having problems, and I made a mistake. But never once did I belittle you when I was with her. And that's why I caved in to her demands. She was going to expose our affair and ruin both of our careers."

Turning to Marlene, Beatrice spits, "You deserve to go to prison again, you witch.'

"Why you old hag!" Marlene screams, moving towards Beatrice. Ronnie jumps out of the way, which brings her nearer to Shark. Zack moves quickly and grabs Marlene before she reaches Beatrice.

Then suddenly there's the sound of glass shattering. Everyone starts scattering about in confusion, trying to get out of the way. A burly man crashes through the sliding door, falls to the floor, then stumbles to his feet. When he reaches for his gun it isn't there.

"Who's this guy?" Alex asks, holding on to Michael.

"He's your bodyguard," Michael says. Alex looks astounded. "I hired him to protect you when all of this started getting out of hand. Now I wish I hadn't," he says, looking over at the burly man.

During the commotion, Shark manages to grab the gun from the floor, and then grabs Ronnie.

"Preston!" Ronnie screams.

Everyone freezes and looks over at Shark, who has an arm around Ronnie's neck and a gun to her head.

"Let her go!" Preston shouts.

Alex steps away from Michael, as if she's going to attack Shark. "Take your hands off my sister, you prick!" she screams, stepping forward.

Marlene looks over at Alex. "So you're another sister," she remarks. "Now I have three of you to take care of."

"Shut up, low-life," Zack commands as Marlene struggles to escape his grip.

Alex continues to move forward until Michael reaches out and grabs her arm, pulling her back. "What do you think you're doing?" he demands.

"I'm going to help my sister. No one else is," she hisses.

"Sweetheart, let Preston and his partner do their job," he begs. Alex snatches her arm from his grip, and looks on as Preston tries to reason with Shark.

"Come on, man," Preston pleads. "Let the lady go."

"I don't think so, my friend. She's my ticket out of here."

"I'm no friend of yours," Preston says, remaining calm. Zack looks over at Preston, knowing he will do whatever it takes to protect Ronnie.

Preston steps forward with his arms straight out from his sides. "See, I have no weapon, Shark. Now send her over to me. She's no good to you anyway, man, and she'll only slow you down."

"Cut the crap," Shark snaps. "I know this is your woman. I saw the look between you two. You need not worry, I won't hurt her. That's the least I can do for you."

Preston looks at Shark, stunned. "For me! You don't even know me."

"That's where you're wrong, my son. I know all about you. I may not have raised you, I left that up to your grandmother. But I've kept track of you over the years."

In a total state of shock, Preston becomes speechless. Even Ronnie quits squirming after that statement. Everyone else looks on in amazement.

All except Zack. "Pres, snap out of it, man! Now is not the time to dwell on the past. Look at him, man! He's ready to walk out that door with someone very precious to you. Just like he walked away years ago, taking away all the precious memories of your mother. Don't let him do it to you twice, Pres."

"Shut up!" Shark shouts. "You don't know what you're talking about! Enough of this shit! Old man," he yells to James, "get my money, now!"

As James gets up, the sound of police sirens is heard. "Move it, old man," Shark snarls.

"Wait!" Preston shouts. "Don't go anywhere, Judge Crawford. Shark, I can't let you do this."

"What are you going to do, kill your own father?" Shark asks sarcastically.

"My father died with my mother years ago," Preston says harshly.

"I'm getting my money, Preston, and I'm walking out of here with this beauty," Shark says. He then points the gun at James' signaling him to get the money. James slowly starts walking over to where he has the money stashed.

Suddenly, voices come blaring out of a bull horn. "This is the FBI. Come out with your hands up!"

"Hurry up, old man!" Shark yells.

James goes to his desk to retrieve a key. He then walks over to a beautiful Van Gogh painting. When he lifts the painting, it exposes a small door. He takes the key and unlocks the door. After opening the door, he pulls out a black leather duffel bag. He then closes the door, locks it, and rearranges the painting to its proper place.

"Give me the bag old man, and your car keys," Shark says menacingly. James moves at a faster pace, until he's close enough to hand Shark the bag and keys. After grabbing the bag, Shark starts backing out of the study, dragging Ronnie along with him.

"What about me, Shark!" Marlene screams.

"Sorry baby, it's been nice," he says moving closer to the front door.

"You bastard!" Marlene screams.

When Shark reaches the door, Preston knows it's time to make his move. He looks over at Zack, then the bodyguard. "Here, take this," Preston says, throwing a second gun he had to the bodyguard. "You're going to need it to watch her."

The bodyguard takes hold of Marlene so Zack can help Preston. The two men both follow Shark with caution.

"This is the FBI," the bull horn announces again. "This is also your last warning. Come out with your hands up, or we will be forced to come in."

Shark opens the door, holding Ronnie in front of him. The officers outside are already in position, ready to fire. Agent Farley and Moss notice instantly that Shark has a hostage. "Hold your fire!" Agent Farley yells to his men.

"I'm coming out, but not alone!" Shark shouts. "You shoot me and she dies too."

"You won't leave here alive, Shark," Farley responds. "So let the lady go."

"I can't do that, fellows," Shark says grimly, dragging Ronnie out the door and towards the car.

"Preston!" Ronnie screams. "Help me!"

Preston and Zack make their way to the door. When Preston sees how close Shark is to getting into the car with Ronnie, he starts moving in closer. "Pres wait!" Zack yells. But Preston keeps on going until he's stopped by a gun pointing straight at him.

"Don't make me do it, son," Shark says softly.

"I'm not your son," Preston responds. "I'm nothing to you."

"That's where you're wrong. I left because I'm no good. Your mother died because of me. I always liked the fast life Preston, and your mother paid for my indiscretions with her life."

"What are you saying? My mother died giving birth to me."

"That's what the old lady wanted you to believe. You were a year or so old when your mother was intentionally run down. Can't you see, I left to protect you. And I couldn't contact you. I was a criminal and you were a cop. That combination don't mix." While talking Shark lets his guard down, and lowers his gun slightly. Preston looks over at Ronnie and knows it's time to strike. It's now or never.

Preston leaps forward onto Shark, causing Ronnie to hit her head on the car, and fall unconscious to the ground. Zack runs out, screaming at the cops not to shoot. Upon hearing the commotion, everyone rushes to the window to see what's going on.

Everyone except Alex. She runs straight out the door, calling out Ronnie's name, with Michael on her heels. Seeing Ronnie on the ground, and Preston struggling with Shark, causes Alex to lose it. She starts screaming while continuing to make her way to Ronnie. Michael finally catches up with her and pulls her back, kicking and fighting him.

Preston and Shark are rolling around on the ground, when Shark discovers the gun to the side of them. Preston notices the gun too and tries to get to it before Shark, but Shark reaches it first.

Shark stands up, unsteady from the struggle, pointing the gun at Preston. Finally Preston makes his way up from the ground and stands, breathing hard.

"I could kill you right now," Shark says, barely able to get the words out from being out of breath. "But I owe your mother." He hesitates for a moment, then continues. "Maybe I'll see you again one day, son." He slowly picks up the duffel bag while still pointing the gun at Preston. He takes a long look at his son, then turns and begins running towards the car.

He never makes it. Shots ring out, and Shark falls to the ground, still holding the duffel bag.

Preston stares for a second at the father he never knew, and never will know. He then runs over to where Ronnie is laying, and calls out for an ambulance, while Agents Farley and Moss walked over to Shark's body.

Zack directs the EMS unit towards Ronnie. It looks like chaos as the police officers scatter about checking out the scene of the crime. Knowing everything is now safe, everyone starts coming out of the house. Alex breaks away from Michael and runs over to Ronnie. By the time Alex reaches the stretcher, Ronnie is regaining consciousness.

"Is she going to be okay?" Alex asks frantically.

"My baby is going to be just fine," Preston says, smiling down at Ronnie. Ronnie looks up at Preston lovingly, while reaching for his hand. "Hey sis," she says weakly to Alex. "Didn't I tell you my baby would rescue us?"

"You were right as usual," Alex says with a smile. Filled with emotions, she turns away so Ronnie won't notice the tears, when a touch on her shoulder makes her jump.

"It's me, sweetheart," a familiar voice says. She turn to find Michael standing behind her.

No words were necessary, or spoken. What she sees in his eyes is enough. The coldness is gone, replaced with love. She throws her arms around him and cries as he holds her tight. They stand embracing as Marlene walks past in handcuffs, escorted by the police.

James and Beatrice look on as they see their son lovingly hold his wife. James kisses Beatrice slightly on her forehead, and both head back inside their home.

"Hey Pres, how are you holding up, man?" Zack asks.

"It's over, man. Now it's time to start rebuilding. Thanks for everything."

"You're my homey," Zack responds. "Pres, I'm outta here. I have a honey waiting on me."

"So do I," Preston says, smiling at Ronnie.

"Take care Ronnie," Zack says, kissing her on the cheek.

"You too," she responds weakly.

Zack slaps Preston on the back and walks away.

"Ready to take a ride, baby?" Preston asks.

"As long as I'm on top," she answers, smiling.

"All banged up and still thinking about sex," he laughs.

After Ronnie is lifted into the ambulance, Preston joins her. Sitting next to Ronnie as she lays on the stretcher, he leans over and gently places a kiss on her forehead.

"Preston," she says softly.

"Yes baby?" he answers with concern.

"Can we please get back to our simple life now?"

Staring into those beautiful eyes he answers, "We sure can. For now on, there will be more loving and less drama."

She looks up at him with a smile, then closes her eyes to the sound of the siren.

The ambulance takes off, with Michael and Alex following closely behind in his father's car. Alex turns to take one last look at the scene, then looks up to the sky.

"Thank you God," she whispers. "Thank you…"

Belinda Walker-Graham

ABOUT THE AUTHOR

Belinda Walker-Graham was born and raised in River Rouge, Michigan. Even as a child she had a vivid imagination, and learned how to place thoughts on paper.

At age 12 she and two other students wrote a play. Her school was so impressed, they closed classes for two hours so Belinda and the students could act the play out. Two other schools were invited.

Graham attended Detroit College of Business and took Management classes, then attended Marygrove college for Management. She has worked for 20 years in the communication field.

Graham also writes poetry, inspired by her experience, and from the heart. Her love of writing inspired her to become a published author. She succeeded with the debut of her first novel.

Graham currently lives in Michigan with her husband, where she is working on her second novel.

www.ingramcontent.com/pod-product-compliance
Lightning Source LLC
Chambersburg PA
CBHW022243290526
45785CB00015B/155